NOTE: This is a pre-production, preview copy of the book.

Praise for *The Dignity Gap*

Well worth your time as Bob winsomely challenges us to honor the God-given dignity of everyone and thus transform our work cultures into creative places of joy. It is a quick read, but one that will inspire you to be a more life-giving friend and colleague.

Pete Howard
Senior Fellow for Transformation, Accord Network
Global Advisor, Caritas In Veritate Intl.

Learning is a journey. In light of this truth, I implore you to slip into your proverbial shoes, grab your pack and water, and allow Bob to take you on an excursion of life-changing discovery. The personal breakthroughs and understanding this book unpacks will have a profound impact in how you view and interact with yourself and others. Bob masterfully illuminates why dignity matters, what it is, and how we can practically live it out.

Pat Mcalla
Executive Director at Operation JOY Foundation
President of Four Thirteen Productions

THE
DIGNITY
GAP

Are You Leading Beyond Diversity and Inclusion?

THE DIGNITY GAP

Are You Leading Beyond Diversity and Inclusion?

BOB FABEY

Free Agent Press
Satsuma, Alabama

The Dignity Gap
Copyright © 2022—Bob Fabey

Published by Free Agent Press

All rights reserved. This book is protected by the copyright laws of the United States of America. This book may not be copied or reprinted for commercial gain or profit. The use of short quotations or occasional page copying for personal or group study is permitted and encouraged. Permission will be granted upon request.

Book Design: James Woosley, FreeAgentPress.com

ISBN: 978-1-946730-25-1 (hardback)
ISBN: 978-1-946730-26-8 (paperback)
ISBN: 978-1-946730-27-5 (ebook)

Cover and Book Design by James Woosley, FreeAgentPress.com

Published by Free Agent Press
FreeAgentPress.com
Satsuma, Alabama 36572
VID: 20221214

*For
Bob and Gretchen*

CONTENTS

Preface xv

Introduction 1

Chapter 1: A Heightened Sense of Things 5

Chapter 2: The Principal Principle 17

Chapter 3: The Dignity Gap 35

Chapter 4: Unleashing the Power 49

Chapter 5: Donna Hicks on Dignity 59

Chapter 6: The Surprising Place of Dignity 77

Chapter 7: The Role of Fear in Dignity 87

Chapter 8: Relate 99

Chapter 9: Insight 113

Chapter 10: Serving 123

Chapter 11: Kindness 129

Chapter 12: Dignity's Power in Story 139

Chapter 13: An Ancient Power 155

Chapter 14: Obstacles to Embracing our Dignity 167

Chapter 15: The Dignity Connection 183

Chapter 16: A Call to Action 191

Conclusion: Becoming a Dignity Champion 205

Author Bio 209

ACKNOWLEDGMENTS

Thanks to the incredible Stanford Public Library. Stanford, MT. A little treasure in central Montana, a writer's gem.

To the many coffee shops who served as a refuge.

Special thanks to Meredith, Chris, and Mat who never burn my espresso shots.

I would also like to add special thanks to Jacqueline Chapman, who provided the editing of my first draft of this book.

Thanks to the many who let me tell their stories.

And to Donna Hicks for her encouragement.

PREFACE

KINDNESS WAS ALWAYS A way forward in my family. We treated others with kindness and helped those around us without hesitation.

However, if someone wronged us, as a family or as individuals, you could quote the movie *Tombstone* when Wyatt Earp (played by Kirk Russell) gave the ominous warning after his brother was shot and killed: "You tell 'em I'm coming, and hell's coming with me, you hear?" My family truly lived at peace, but we were ready to pay people back for the evil or pain they visited upon us. Most of this came from my dad, but my mom, though tiny, was a force to be reckoned with as all mamma bears are.

Maybe you grew up the same way or still live that way: Be nice to those who are nice but stick to the jerks who deserve it.

The problem is, we all deserve to have it stuck to us at some point. All of us have done things that deserve someone's wrath.

Which means we have a few options in choosing how we live: (1) We can stick it to everyone who deserves it; (2) we can overlook the pain and evil that comes to us from others; or (3) we can find an authentically human way forward—we can choose to validate one another's dignity.

As a pastor, I have listened to thousands of stories from kids and adults about how others have violated their dignity over and over; in fact, that's the reason many people come to me. People have treated them like objects, and eventually the natural outworking of those experiences becomes evident. In all of it there is pain, evil, and ugliness, and I am asked to help people work through that.

From grade school through high school, I was relentlessly picked on. A handful of kids made my life hell because they didn't like me. They didn't like how I acted. They didn't like how I looked (I had a HUGE overbite). They didn't like anything about me, and there was nothing I could do about it. That objectification wasn't fun.

I have noticed that same objectification in the work world. In many workplaces, an employee is nothing more than a cog in the machine. She isn't a person; he's only a number; and they're both sales figures and a bottom line. Employees are only as good as the last thing they produced. If they don't produce, they're out, replaced by someone who can do better. That's just how the world works. Right?

On the surface that appears true, but there is another current. No one treats their spouses this way. No one treats their kids this way (or if they do, they get in loads of trouble). It isn't human; it's subhuman. It's below us to act this way.

So why do we do it? Why do we treat people like objects?

For years, I have used a Rubik's Cube in my talks to make my point: We can't twist and manipulate people into what we want, especially because none of us are perfect and none of us have all our "sides" together. Those who attempt to manipulate the "cube" will find employees leaving en masse. Those who objectify the squares on the "cube" at school will find themselves alone. The same at home. No one enjoys being manipulated or objectified.

Efforts in the workplace and schools to ensure such objectification and manipulation do not happen include diversity programs or policies of inclusion to create places where people feel safe, honored, and valued for who they are. But their efforts can only go so far; programs and policies can only do so much.

The ultimate answer to this issue: persons treating other persons with dignity. Yes to diversity, yes to inclusion, but validating the dignity a person *already* possesses is of the highest human virtue. A school, workplace, home—*any space* that makes the choice to honor a person's dignity means that all people win because *dignity wins*.

I'm a people champion and I believe in the potential of every single person. When people are treated with dignity and validate their own dignity, they are capable of a great many things. When we treat others with dignity, we see our family, friends, and coworkers not as problems to be solved, but as potential to be realized. Each person adds a unique contribution to our world, and we are to be the people who help each other find those contributions. Judgments and attitudes that hold us back and keep others down pervade our culture. We can be free from those.

You can be the reason someone wins at life. You can be the reason someone excels at work. Because you know and celebrate the power of dignity.

INTRODUCTION

ONE ADVANTAGE TO MY line of work is that I get to talk with your people. I listen to what your people say about you. I listen to what they say about the workplace you create. I hear about how you handle stress, problems, and opportunities. They tell me about what you say and how you act, and about who gets treated well and who doesn't. I hear about what you like and what you don't like. I hear about what vacations you will approve, and about how you make your people feel when they take one. It isn't easy to be in business today.

To be sure, there are *at least* two sides to every story, and I am not so naive as to believe everything I am told without hesitation, but people share and I pay attention.

And what am I hearing?

People are tired.

People are tired of being treated like objects. People are tired of not being supported. Employees are looking for more than a paycheck and they're looking outside your organization. Gone are the days when bonuses, salaries, and vacations were enough to keep people around. They want to know they are valued and valuable, not just because they fulfill their job description, but beyond that. They want to know they are participating in something worthwhile. They want to be a part of something bigger than themselves. They want to grow. They want to know their lives outside the workplace matter, and they are looking to you and their work environments to provide *all* this.

This is a tall task for any work environment, especially for those who have no idea how to value people in these crucial areas. And you may be a people leader who is looking for the exact same things.

What can we do?

Some companies respond by creating policies and programs, which tend to look like rules and regulations around diversity or inclusion. They seek to even the playing field for everyone and ensure that no one is mistreated. Such policies and programs are helpful and necessary on many levels, but they often fall short.

Why?

Because rules and policies don't offer practical, proactive ways to treat people (including yourself!) in ways that transform teams and individuals. Productivity is linked to how people *feel.* We are human beings, not human doings. How people feel and what they think are important. Therefore, the environments we create either help others flourish or limit them in critical ways.

In this book, you will find ways to help your people flourish. You will learn how to overcome the objectification so prevalent in today's workplace. You will discover practical ways to honor and validate the dignity of everyone in your charge.

By learning about and practicing the celebration of dignity, you will become a people champion. And then when they come to me, everything the people you champion tell me will be good or better (though maybe not perfect). They will beam with joy as they talk about how valued and important they feel at work, and how they love bringing that excitement to others. They will tell me how they've changed and how the workplace has changed, for the better. They will talk about how *dignity wins*, and so will you.

CHAPTER 1
A Heightened Sense of Things
Why We're Ready to Spring

AFTER A LONG DRIVE with close attention paid to icy roads and poor driving conditions, I was tired. We had arrived at my in-laws' ranch, thirteen miles into the mountains, outside a town of five hundred people, much later than I'd wanted and well after dark. It was pitch black outside. The stars were crisp and clear, and sound only traveled a few feet in the snow. Central Montana has a way of making one feel small and alone when outside in wintertime.

Excited to have finished driving and to see family, we hurried inside for a few moments of greeting and settling in.

Needing to retrieve our bags from the vehicle, I stepped out into the cold dark, a stark contrast from the warmth of the house with beautiful fire and soft light. Those familiar with winter in the north know that sometimes snow can develop a crust in which the top layer is solid for a moment before it breaks to reveal a soft underbelly. It has an eerie quality to it.

To say I was afraid to go back out into the dark and the cold to get our things would be incorrect. I was wary. The bears were asleep, so no big deal, but there are cougars around, and I'm not so fond of cats. Cats *plus* the fact that we are a long way from the next ranch and I know too much about the Manson family, well, it's fair that I was feeling nervous, right?

Growing up, I read Louis L'Amour books about the West and about what it took to live in an untamed land. His characters and descriptions of life in the West taught me two lessons. First, I should never sit with my back to the entrance of the saloon (or restaurant as saloons are harder to find these days). My back to the door means I can't see the room well, nor can I see who comes in. Cowboy or not, it's a bad idea for anyone expecting trouble who needs to be aware of their surroundings. Secondly, I learned I should not look directly into a fire at night. While beautiful and comforting, looking into the fire would blind me; once I look away from the fire, I can't see into the dark and don't know who or what is sneaking up on me. For a cowboy, that could mean death. For me, it would probably mean far less.

My brain was on high alert as I went outside to get our things.

I walked across the driveway and into the snow. In the hollow silence the sound dropped a few feet from its origin. I opened the trunk, and the noise it made felt like a violation. The assist light came on and I could easily see our things. I grabbed the suitcases and bags, placed them in the snow, and prepared to shut the trunk.

It was then I realized: I broke rule number two. I hadn't stared into the flames of a fire, but I did look at a lighted area. I had even looked directly at the light bulb in the trunk.

It took me a moment to get my bearings as I looked into the dark for our bags.

I was blind.

My eyes adjusted as I closed the trunk and reached for our suitcases.

But then it happened.

Out in the dark, just within sight, mortal eyes glaring with rage reached out and pierced my soul. Fangs bared from an open mouth to tear my flesh, claws extended to rip me apart. My heart stopped for a moment as a roar hit my ears.

I knew I was dead.

How Our Brains Work

Our brains do funny things in moments like these. The limbic system, designed to help us at such times, kicks in. Our bodies flood with hormones and stimulants meant to help us flee the danger or fight it—the fight-or-flight response. Some people set their jaws, clench their fists, dig in their heels, and take a swing. Others have the quick-twitch muscle response, recoil from the danger, and move away as fast as possible, like retracting a hand from a hot stove. Both reactions happen in a moment and can be credited with keeping humans alive since the dawn of time. These are primitive, instinctual responses without much cognition happening.

We may not know the exact reason that causes someone's fight-or-flight or quick-recoil response to kick in. For example, we encounter an angry person who looks ready to fight for no apparent reason, or someone suddenly cuts off communication with us without giving an explanation. There may be valid reasons for people behaving this way, and their actions may well be a cognitive choice.

While the background may be unclear to us, what is clear in moments like these is that people are in a heightened state of awareness. They read cues that tell them danger is near or all around. Their friends and family, social media, the news, and other inputs tell them to be aware and concerned about a great many things. They begin to feel that they can't trust people, that systems are out to get them, and that every day is a fight for survival. Suddenly everything puts them on alert: ready to fight or ready to run or ready to recoil.

So it is for all of us. If we are all exposed and vulnerable in ways we don't choose, then in some way, we are victims of our own existence. We are uncertain of how we will experience one another, and so become vigilant or even jaded. Whatever naivety we still have disappears unless we decide to do something differently.

How can we live in a world where people are poised to spring, and the tensions for fight-or-flight are real? They are in all of us. That tension exists in all of us. How can we possibly respond to one another in such a tenuous environment? What can we do at home, at play, or in the workplace to help ease the tension and find a way forward?

Back to that dark, silent night in Montana. Seeing my imminent demise in the fangs, claws, and eyes lunging out of the darkness, I did exactly what my brain told me to do.

I responded the way my limbic system was designed: I froze and fell.

That's right. I fell over like a fainting goat and collapsed in the snow next to the car.

What appeared out of the dark wasn't a member of a satanic cult or a cougar. To my great humiliation, it was my wife. She hid in the dark, waiting to scare me. And scare me she did. Her laughter pierced the air as she came into view, bent over double in spasms of joy and hilarity. I, however, was lying in the snow, wondering if my heart was still beating, and trying to come to terms with the fact that I was still alive.

I will never live this down.

What happened was important for a few reasons. First, I was ready for something to happen. The situation was ripe for danger. My mind was already at work, concerned for my safety entering an environment that left me vulnerable. It was dark, I was tired, and we were miles from others in the dead of winter. My brain was on high alert.

This happens a lot. There's a dreaded meeting or conversation to have or a party to attend, situations that cause us concern and open us up to any adverse outcomes that might occur. We become wary, and our limbic system kicks into high gear.

When I froze and collapsed, I didn't fight and I didn't run. My body seized and sort of shut down. What's interesting to note: this has happened to me on other occasions. Unexpectedly scared, my legs melted from under me. Far from ready to fight and certainly not ready for flight, I drop like a wet rag. There is nothing cognitive about my initial reaction.

It is impossible to know how people will respond to their environments and their stimulus. The hormones and chemicals racing through their bodies are designed to keep them safe, and their limbic system response may make them ready to fight and appear angry. Running works the same way; everything inside them tells them they must get to safety. When we encounter someone who appears angry or scared, we are experiencing their need to be safe. Their primitive protection system is kicking in. Will they take off running, will they swing their fists, or will they seize? It isn't cognitive, its chemical. There isn't a lot of thought going on beyond changing the state of the encounter.

This isn't a fun experience for most. People feel out of control and like someone else was in control in that moment. That increases the likelihood that they will act strongly. They don't like what happened before, it is now happening again, and they got ready to spring determined to stop it this time.

How can we live together in this uncertainty?

How I responded to my initial reaction is critical. After collecting the shattered pieces of my ego from the crusty snow, my adrenaline died down, and I laughed. It was hilarious; my wife got me good. She loves to tell this story and giggles every time she does.

Some fears are genuine though. Not all situations turn out safely or become a good story. Some create deep wounds that last, leaving scars that tell terrible stories. When I think about my response, I'd love to say I was ready to fight and take on my terrible fear, but I wasn't. I'd love to say I sprang out of danger's way like a springbuck from the jaws of a crocodile at the watering hole, but I didn't.

I could easily call myself a coward or repeat other negative thoughts to myself. I could play the times I've dropped to the ground over and over and tell myself that I'd be useless in a moment of need. But that isn't who I am because I can get up and respond well when my cognition returns.

We move past our initial fight, flight, or collapse responses. Life moves on. We have other experiences and create stories to tell—some fighting, some fleeing, and some falling. We get opportunities to learn and grow in every instance. With each interaction, we have the chance to choose how we will respond.

With each interaction, we have the chance to choose how we will respond.

Our workplaces and our relationships in them encompass a large part of our lives. In the space and time dedicated to our workplace, we encounter many of these opportunities. We have the chance to embrace the fight-or-flight moments and learn to grow past them. Coworkers, managers, directors, and bosses all have a sense of what is happening around them. They all are attuned to circumstances in the office. They will be ready to respond. Because they are all trying to stay safe but still connect, and so are you and I.

Harvard professor and researcher, Donna Hicks writes in her book *Dignity: Its Essential Role in Resolving Conflict*:

> Importantly, however, we also have the power within us to make different choices about how we react to instincts…. The limbic system in our brain, the one that prompts the fight-or-flight reaction and the attendant emotions, promotes survival in another way: it encourages humans to get close to one another, to connect.[1]

Two things happen in the limbic system at the same time: We want to get away, and we want to connect. Perhaps connecting is a way of staying safe, but it seems that many feel the best way to stay safe is through disconnection.

What are we to do in the moment when our choices are fight, flight, freeze, or even connection? We need to move past our initial limbic system response to something deeper and more meaningful.

And what do we do when we reach safety or connection?

How do we live once the fear subsides, the hand is pulled from the stove, or we pick ourselves up from the snow?

We live in dignity.

Dignity for others and dignity for ourselves.

What Is Dignity?

Dignity means that despite race, creed, gender, or any other marker that identifies a person, every human being is valuable. Hicks says it this way: "Dignity is a birthright. We have little trouble seeing this when a child is born; there is no question about children's value and worth. If only we could hold onto this truth about human beings

---
1 – Donna Hicks Ph D, *Dignity: Its Essential Role in Resolving Conflict* (Yale University Press, 2013), Page 8.

as they grow into adults, if only we could continue to feel their value, then it would be so much easier to treat them well and keep them safe from harm. Treating others with dignity, then, becomes the baseline for our interactions. We must treat others as if they matter, as if they are worthy of care and attention."[2]

Dignity implies a two-fold response: a belief in the inherent worth of every human being and action based on that belief.

After WWII, much of Europe was in tatters. Infrastructure lay in ruins, millions were dead, and rubble was everywhere. The European nations needed a way forward as independent societies and as a whole—as neighbors and friends. The Universal Declaration of Human Rights was adopted to help accomplish this vital work. On December 10, 1948, a unanimous vote was taken, and all but Soviet Bloc countries and a few others who abstained from voting adopted the declaration. The first article reads: "All human beings are born free and equal in dignity and rights. They are endowed with reason and conscience and should act towards one another in a spirit of brotherhood."[3]

From at least 1948, there has been a public understanding of dignity that looks like these definitions. Some have argued that the idea of dignity came in the mid-1780s with Kant, while others trace its roots back further. In the book *Dignity: A History*,[4] an effort is made to trace the roots of dignity in order to discover where the idea

---

2 – Donna Hicks Ph D, *Dignity: Its Essential Role in Resolving Conflict* (Yale University Press, 2013), Page 4.

3 – The Universal Declaration of Human Rights, Article 1.

4 – Remy Debes, *Dignity: A History* (Oxford University Press, Incorporated, 2017).

came from. Moving from ancient Greece through Rome, through Christianity, Buddhism, and Islam, scholars from various disciplines tackle the notion from their perspective. In such an attempt, one can imagine missing various points that may help find the origin or, at least, give an example we could use to see what dignity looks like today. Indeed, there isn't much mention of Judaism and its role, and a closer look at Christianity may produce a more profound sense of connection to dignity and the image of God than the book provides.

If people are unable to contribute to society, do they have value? If people's only value is to contribute economically, to provide a good or service that keeps the system moving forward, we are in deep trouble. People are more than their contributions, and a belief that people bear the image of God despite their actions, abilities, or potential can have a massive impact for good.

As such, the definition of dignity in this book is: People have inherent value. Period.

This idea isn't without problems. It isn't as if we speak the word *dignity* and everything is magically better. Dignity presents some issues as well. If we argue for the inherent worth of every human being, then we must look at the good ones *and* the bad ones. It's easy to take people like Jesus (whom we will look at later), Mother Teresa, Nelson Mandela, or Dr. Martin Luther King, Jr. and say they are people worthy of dignity. What about the Stalins, Maos, and Hitlers of the world? What about people who perpetrate crimes against children? In fact, the proponents of dignity are often violators of the very dignity they champion. It's an unfortunate truth that religious organizations and institutions of higher learning are not exempt. How can that be?

As Hicks pointed out, dignity is a birthright. Respect is behavior-based and earned. No one likes to hear that, but there is an important distinction to be made. We are not the sum of our actions, and our identity is not solely found in our behaviors. We are more than that. Dignity means that people who may not be worthy of respect are worthy of dignity. If a behavior is contrary to humanity, if it is sub-human, it isn't worthy of respect. That's how we can talk about someone's behavior without violating their dignity.

Dignity is an idea and a belief that challenges how we view others and how we view ourselves. We are like Dr. Doolittle's Pushmi-Pullyu (pronounced "push-me-pull-you"), two-headed and maybe a bit stubborn; we can believe one thing and act out another. One could rightly question whether we believe when we act to the contrary: Do people who violate the dignity of others really believe in dignity? Of course they do. Imperfection doesn't mean we can't have dignity as a goal and a guidepost. We walk a fine line with dignity. It is ours to embrace and celebrate as well as ours to violate and deface.

To move past our initial responses and into a new (maybe not entirely new) way of being connected, we must choose common ground. I believe that common ground is our humanity. Having traveled the globe, I have found the people of Central Asia aren't all that different from the people of East Africa. Alaskans aren't all that different from Floridians. Russians aren't all that different from Americans. We are people. We love, we eat, we laugh, we cry. We are brothers and sisters, moms and dads. If you are human, you possess dignity. To be human = dignity. How we got here, whether through evolution or religious belief systems, dignity is the way forward for us. Why? Because even as imperfect as we are, *dignity wins*.

CHAPTER 2
The Principal Principle
Principled People Living Principled Lives

I SAT IN THE JUNIOR high school hallway, noticing how the light reflected off the newly polished floor. No students were walking by, and no teachers were rushing to their classrooms. The hallway was empty, except for me. I was sitting outside of my math class. I often sat outside of my math class as I'd been kindly asked to leave the room. I can still hear my teacher: "Mr. Fabey, out in the hall and do it now. Please." Remembering the sound of his vocal inflections still makes me flinch.

I stared at the lockers, tracing my eye up and down the gray paint, noticing the dents and imperfections as I went. When I grew bored doing that, I looked at my shoes and tapped my feet together as I thought about how bad it sucked sitting all alone in the hall. My musings were occasionally interrupted by a student with a hall pass for the bathroom. Their glance said it all: *You cause problems.* It was always a glance, I assume, so that they wouldn't get in trouble as well.

Sometimes, a classroom door opened, and a friend came out. Which was a different experience entirely. They looked around quickly to find where I was sitting, their laughter and smile making light of the fact that I was in trouble. They usually said something like, "Dude! I can't believe he kicked you out!" I responded with something like, "I know! What a jerk!" Then off they went, walking down the hall.

But the most terrifying thing while sitting in the hallway was hearing footsteps.

The sound of footsteps produced anxiety and regret; undoubtedly, that was the effect the teacher who sent me to the hallway wanted to create.

Footsteps echoing down those polished tile floors were the sound of death and inevitability. I was so terrified because I didn't know whose footsteps they belonged to. I would only know once the person rounded the corner. Were they the footsteps of a friend who, when they turned the corner, would smile and laugh? Were they the footsteps of a fellow student whose eyes would quickly divert? Or was it the worst possible set of footsteps: our principal, Mr. Smith? (I changed his name to protect the innocent.)

Mr. Smith invoked a kind of dread only a junior high student can feel when faced with their principal. He was larger than life. I recall his rounded shoulders and slightly stooped frame partially blocked the light in the hallway. It felt apocalyptic. The light seemed to diminish as the sound of his footsteps approached. He wore slacks and cardigans.

His glasses looked as if he was born with them, and as crazy as it sounds, his hair was so gray it had a blue tint. I'm sure he wasn't a bad man. I know some people who knew and loved him, and he was probably the life of the party in other settings. But for a seventh grader sitting in the hallway because his behavior was less than stellar, Mr. Smith was the incarnation of doom.

Anyone who had the pleasure of being called into his office would notice the paddle strategically placed on the wall just behind his desk and above his head. One might think it reminded Mr. Smith of when he survived forty days on a life raft in the middle of the ocean. Or maybe he was a sea captain in a former life or a fisherman from the Northeast who could regale you with tales in Hemingwayesque fashion. Alas, it was not that kind of paddle. This paddle was modified with a shorter handle to improve the swing. It was not designed to cut through the water; it was designed to slice through the air…fast. The paddle had a much smaller face, made for the sole purpose of punishment, and it looked effective. Finally, the paddle had holes in it. Holes! Many of us surmised it was to keep the swing from slowing down when swatting an out-of-hand youngster. Imagine a whistle coming from those holes as it approached your backside. Terrifying.

Mr. Smith (and perhaps that paddle) proved to be what students oriented themselves around every day. When he was in the halls, students grew quiet and stood still in line outside the classrooms. We waited for the previous class to get out without the usual joking, pushing, and shoving. When he was on the school radio, we listened carefully. Just invoking his name produced any number of reactions. Announcing his approach or telling others that so-and-so went to his office created everything from terror to funeral arrangements.

Mr. Smith embodied the principal principle. His presence made everything work a certain way. That's how principals work. Whether behind the scenes or up front, principals provide a context where teachers thrive, staff develops, and students learn, and how they do it is part of the magic of leadership and influence. That's one thing you will hear throughout this book: *How* we do what we do is as important as what we do. To put it in another way, the how is as important as the what.

From my perspective, Mr. Smith's way of doing things was through fear and intimidation. And depending on his goals it worked. If keeping kids from stepping out of line and acting out was his goal, it worked. If making sure there was a veneer of civility at our school, it worked. If making sure students respected the office of the principal, it worked.

However, this type of leadership doesn't necessarily work in many essential areas today. For one, many find it unthinkable that a principal would paddle a child in school today. Parents themselves are even slow to discipline in this manner. Fear and intimidation are not what we want our kids to experience as they attend school. We want them to flourish, to enjoy being kids, and to enjoy learning without the fear of discipline by paddle. We hope that kids orient positively to authority and not see it as negative. We want them to be who they are and to have that celebrated by principals, teachers, and staff.

Just because Mr. Smith's method worked, that doesn't make it the best, still he functioned in two key ways. He was the principal, *and* he was the principle. His title was principal. He oversaw all the faculty and staff, and he had oversight of budgets, the vision for the school, and goals for each year. He was also the principle. He embodied the rules and doctrines that governed our school. Everything oriented around Mr. Smith.

The Principles of Principals

In today's world, we still have both. CEOs, vice presidents, and managers are principals. Positionally in the workplace they hold the greater amount of authority and responsibility. Within that position the workplace may then operate by the principal's way and that is an organizing principle.

Principles are funny things. They can be stated, laminated, framed, and hung on walls. Or they can remain unstated while everyone is still expected to learn and know them. There are fewer things as frustrating in the workplace than the latter.

Maybe you've seen something like this play out before: John who is new to the company is excited about the advance in his career. He is hardworking and dependable. He has kept his head down and steadily climbed the corporate ladder. While things may not have always gone his way, this new job has set the stage for the rest of his career.

The people at his job are friendly and help him in his role as he assesses the needs he will try to meet. However, he keeps hearing about one of his colleagues. As he asks questions about his predecessor and how things work, he keeps hearing Julie's name come up. Julie has been at the company for fifteen years. She is excellent at her job and demands the same from others. She is happy in her role, but those who work under her seem less so. He considers making certain changes but keeps hearing about how Julie would be "upset" if he did so, and he is advised not to do things that may anger Julie. Stories then unfold of Julie's outbursts and red-faced meetings. Her anger is legendary.

After a few months in his new role, John realizes that a large part of the organization is limited because it orients around Julie and her behavior. Nothing is written down. No one has a plaque on the wall, but everyone knows the rules—and not upsetting Julie is rule number one.

When a principal person embodies a toxic principle, the organization is heading for a cliff.

Principles (and principals!) like this can kill a company. When a principal person embodies a toxic principle, the organization is heading for a cliff. Nothing will chase off good people faster than the acceptance of toxic behavior. In fact, according to a Harvard Business School study, getting rid of a toxic individual can benefit a company in savings by more than double over "a superstar performer—one that models desired values and delivers consistent performance."[5]

Getting positively principled people in principal positions is critical because organizations orient around both the principals and the principles. The principal's principles matter. That is what this book is about: Principal people

---

5 – Nicole Torres, "It's Better to Avoid a Toxic Employee than Hire a Superstar," Harvard Business Review, December 9, 2015, https://hbr.org/2015/12/its-better-to-avoid-a-toxic-employee-than-hire-a-superstar.

embodying and championing a fundamental principle—dignity. Again, dignity is the inherent worth of every human being. When principal people embody dignity as a principle, others flourish. Organizations in which employees feel valued are the places where everyone wants to work, and managers who consistently validate the dignity of their employees are the ones everyone wants to work for.

Dignity is the most significant factor in bringing people together. It is the everyday glue of our humanity, from Asia to Africa, from CEO's office to sanitation department. When dignity is valued, people thrive. In an article for Gallup, Ryan Pendell interviewed some of the world's best managers, and one key to their success was caring about employees as real people. "Several managers mentioned that being successful as a manager means thinking beyond the workplace: 'You're there for them if they have a sick child or a sick parent. I think a lot of people outside of management don't realize the impact we make on their lives, dealing with all the experiences beyond the job.' Another sales manager described her vision when she started: 'I committed to my team when I started…I want to help you build the best life you can.'"[6] That goes way beyond the job description; that is what dignity does.

Nothing will chase off good people faster than the acceptance of toxic behavior.

---

[6] – Ryan Pendell, "8 Behaviors of the World's Best Managers," Gallup.com, December 30, 2019, https://www.gallup.com/workplace/272681/habits-world-best-managers.aspx.

Perhaps you don't see yourself as a principal person. I beg to differ. Organizations give titles and authority to people out of necessity, but principals are simply people with influence. Organizationally, you may have a small area of responsibility, but you still have an impact. The way you conduct yourself in the meetings and the break rooms matters. People are watching and listening. They want to know what kind of person you are, what type of character you possess. How you treat those in less authoritative positions than you matters. How you interact with your colleagues matters. Fred Rogers famously said, "Who you are inside is what helps you make and do everything in life."[7] Each of these interactions gives you influence and makes you a principal person. If your nose is in your phone every day when you pass security without paying any attention to them, they will likely form an opinion about you in a given direction. You aren't letting them know they matter or that you think they have value. Walking into a building and saying "hi" to the guard each day makes a significant difference. Asking them how their day is going and wanting to hear the answer provides meaning. They feel like they matter, and you become a principal person because they've given you that place in their world.

When principal people embody dignity as a principle, others flourish.

---

7 – Fred Rogers, *The World According to Mister Rogers: Important Things to Remember* (Hachette Books, 2019).

The Dignity Principle?

We all have principles. They're simply the ideas and beliefs we organize our lives around. They're the foundation of our worldview.

Some people are described as principled, meaning they have strong standards to which they adhere. High-level athletes tend to be very principled people. They have a goal, and to reach that goal, they are careful about how they eat, what they drink, how often they train, and how much sleep they get. The goal in their mind gives orientation to the rest of their lives that looks like discipline. Olympic-level athletes must be principled because their competition will be.

Then there's you and I. We don't have that same set of principles. We are not seen as highly disciplined or certainly not as highly disciplined as an Olympic athlete. If you spent time in the military, you appreciate how principled you had to be to participate in that endeavor. Maybe you still do your running and push-ups, though most likely discontinued those principles once you completed your service. For most of us, we can be principled for a time, but when the season or reason for it ends, we change our thinking and behavior.

It could also be that we are principled people, just not in the same way as the disciplined athlete. Let's look at an example: Hannah likes her work as a receptionist. She enjoys being the "frontline" person for the company and making people feel comfortable and at ease when they visit. She is warm and friendly, thoughtful, and quick to smile. She thinks it dreadful should someone have a lousy experience engaging with her or the company. One of her principles is that everyone that walks through her doors matters. Whether an employee or a client, CEO or cleaning staff, Hannah wants them to hear a kind greeting and find a cheerful attitude. Hannah is also a bit messy. Her systems are piling systems, not filing systems. She is not particularly fit physically and follows no set exercise routine. However, she is an incredibly principled person. Her principles are as strong as anyone's; they just don't look the same.

We all have principles, and they are likely quite strong. We orient around things we like and believe, and it can be difficult to move us from those. The question isn't if we are principled people; the question is what we are principled about. You can be principled about a great many things: how you handle your money, what you do with your body, how you view your career, and how you raise your kids. The argument of this book is for a principle around dignity: Why dignity, and what is it? A fundamental understanding and application of dignity in our lives, at play and at work is a game-changer.

A glance at the news or your favorite social media feed will tell you something. There is an increasing polarization happening, not just in America but around the world. Black or white thinking is popping up in every aspect of society, and the beauty and complexity of what it means to be human are eclipsed by "this" or "that" thinking. There is little room for gray.

According to a recent poll conducted by Public Religion Research Institute (PRRI) and quoted by Alexa Lardieri of *US News & World Report,* "When it comes to political division, 74 percent say the country is very divided. There is little difference among the political parties, with 96 percent of Republicans and 91 percent of Democrats agreeing."[8] You can feel it. You can hear it when talking with your co-workers and family members. Social and political issues are the litmus tests to see where someone lands in the divide. A person is either Republican or Democrat, and once that is established, that knowledge puts that person in a box. If someone doesn't fall into one of those two categories, and they don't have strong feelings about one or more of the critical social issues we face, they are likely dismissed altogether.

In his article posted on *Social Media Today*, Andrew Hutchinson states that Facebook has reached over 2.37 billion users.[9] That is just over thirty percent of the world's population! Over two billion people are connected on a social network that allows them to gain "friends" who are like them or hold similar interests. They share stories, anecdotes, and posts (whether they are true or not) that they find meaningful. People like and share those items and as they do, they bolster their beliefs and principles. In the worst-case scenario, Facebook then becomes an echo chamber, a place where people only hear and reinforce their opinions and beliefs. Soon, people come to believe that "everyone" agrees with "me." Except the "everyone" is merely the ones that person has connected with on Facebook, a tiny portion of actual users. According to an article by Kit Smith, the average profile has 338 "friends."

---

8 – Robert P. Jones and Maxine Najle. "American Democracy in Crisis: The Fate of Pluralism in a Divided Nation." PRRI. https://www.prri.org/research/american-democracy-in-crisis-the-fate-of-pluralism-in-a-divided-nation/ (accessed March 8, 2022).

9 – Andrew Hutchinson. "Facebook Reaches 2.38 Billion Users, Beats Revenue Estimates in Latest Update." Social Media Today. https://www.socialmediatoday.com/news/facebook-reaches-238-billion-users-beats-revenue-estimates-in-latest-upda/553403/ (accessed March 8, 2022).

That certainly isn't "everyone," but to many people, that's how it feels. Which creates a terrible dynamic. What we see, hear, and consume becomes increasingly narrow in scope. We only hear and see what we want, further deepening our beliefs and solidifying our principles, no matter what they are. When we encounter someone who thinks differently or acts differently, we automatically make them the "other." They become "one of them." This is not a helpful dynamic in any area of our lives, especially work.

Furthermore, like some of the propaganda from the early 1900s, we are led to believe that those who disagree with us, wherever they land on the spectrum, are not valuable. People lump one another into giant buckets and treat each other accordingly: They couldn't possibly be intelligent because they don't agree with us, and every intelligent person agrees with us (science proves it by some random internet-based "fact" inserted here). People with real jobs agree with us, so that farmer who works the land doesn't count because he doesn't trust the people with the real jobs. And the people of the Midwest are all just backward because they don't live in the "real world" (as if a fake world exists); what happens in the big cities on the coasts, that's what is real.

Workplaces are filled with people who are not like you, and most agree to a detente because their principles force them to—being more concerned with their paycheck or healthcare benefits than being infected with a coworker's political or social agenda. We co-exist in an in-between space at work for the sake of our principles. Outside of work, though, it's back to our corners. This polarization is harmful and dangerous. What we know about societies that allow the demonetization of groups is not good. History tells us time and time again how ugly this becomes. There must be a different way forward.

Enter dignity. Dignity means that each person, regardless of their ability to produce, contribute, advance, or compete, is valuable. It means that people are noble even when they don't know it or act to the contrary. Dignity implies a worthiness that goes beyond pragmatism and calls us to act accordingly. What would it look like if we treated one another with dignity? How different would our lives look if our interactions with one another were bathed in dignity? It would transform our workspaces. People would feel valued and safe.

A worldwide poll conducted by Georgetown professor Christine Porath found that "employees who felt respected by their leaders reported 56% better health and well-being, 89% greater enjoyment and satisfaction, 92% greater focus and prioritization, 26% more meaning and significance, and 55% more engagement. Being treated with respect had a more powerful effect on employees than other more celebrated leadership behaviors, including recognition and appreciation, communicating an inspiring vision, providing useful feedback—even opportunities for learning, growth, and development. The research shows that employees desperately want to feel respected and valued by their leaders. Yet the majority of people polled reported that they don't regularly receive the respect they seek."[10]

In the same study, nearly half of employees "decreased [their] work effort" and intentionally spent less time at work. Thirty-eight percent "intentionally decreased" the

---

10 – Christin Porath and Douglas R. Conant. "The Key to Campbell Soup's Turnaround? Civility." Harvard Business Review. https://hbr.org/2017/10/the-key-to-campbell-soups-turnaround-civility (accessed March 8, 2022).

quality of their work. Twenty-five percent of employees who had been treated with incivility admitted to taking their frustrations out on customers. Twelve percent left their jobs due to uncivil treatment.[11]

Dignity can solve these problems. Imagine workplaces where people are valued, where they worked harder, treated customers with kindness, and stayed at jobs, preventing the need to train and onboard new employees. Organizations would work to invest in worker's success, not just as an employee but as a person. For example, companies could talk about behaviors instead of placing people into boxes or lumping others into categories.

You cannot have inclusion without dignity.

You cannot have belonging without dignity.

Dignity is a missing ingredient in many workplaces. Businesses and organizations get caught up in ensuring they check the boxes of diversity and inclusion, but they miss the point. Yes, diversity is critical. We must have a variety of voices from different people in decision-making and culture creation. For too long, people of color or other minorities have not had a voice at the table, and

---

11 – Marissa Levin. "Harvard Research Proves Toxic Employees Destroy Your Culture and Your Bottom Line." Inc. https://www.inc.com/marissa-levin/harvard-research-proves-toxic-employees-destroy-your-culture-your-bottom-line.html (accessed March 8, 2022).

women do deserve equal treatment across the board. Inclusion is an integration of diversity. I've heard it said that diversity is getting a ticket to the dance, and inclusion is being asked out on the floor." You cannot have inclusion without dignity. You cannot have belonging without dignity. Dignity softens the heart and mind. It moves us from being unwilling participants in the dance to co-creators in beauty. It doesn't matter if a person identifies as a man or woman, non-binary, gay, straight, and anywhere in between. It doesn't matter if someone is single or married. It doesn't matter what race, creed, or economic status they are. Dignity makes the dance beautiful and joy-filled for everyone involved.

Everyone starts at the same place: human. In the workplace, despite different roles, titles, paychecks, or responsibilities, everyone is worthy. I will say more about this later, but for now, I want to emphasize the idea that principal people (that's you because you're reading this) acting in a principled way is how we move forward and how dignity wins.

> Dignity softens the heart and mind. It moves us from being unwilling participants in the dance to co-creators in beauty.

The cost of not upholding dignity in others equals loss in energy, time, relationships, and money. Businesses cannot continue to create environments where people are objectified and still hope to compete in the global marketplace. Some workspaces and leaders are taking this issue seriously while others are falling behind. The next chapter helps us examine the growing problem and points us toward a hopeful future.

My behavior in junior high landed me in the hallway. It happened on more than one occasion. Was I a bad kid? Was I a problem to be fixed? What needed to change was my behavior and a sense of my own dignity.

Those shiny halls have helped me better understand who I was and who I am today. So did Mr. Jones. He was a science teacher who, on occasion, sent me to the hallway. In what became a critical moment for me, although I wouldn't fully realize the impact for some time, he made me do a little assignment. He asked me to take out a piece of notepaper and draw a line down the middle. On the left, list all the things I liked about myself, and on the right, list all the things I didn't like.

I started to write. The list on the left was short. Really short. On the right, the list grew and grew.

When I finished, Mr. Jones pulled out another piece of paper. It was his list. But it was not a list about him; it was his list for me. On the right were only a few items. But on the left, the side that described what he liked about me, the list was long, much longer than mine.

I don't remember what was on the list, but I do remember it was tough to take in. Mostly I just remember that Mr. Jones was validating my dignity. He attacked the problem, not the person. He responded to who I was, not just my behavior. He saw far beyond the angry, confused, scared kid who used humor to make his way through school.

Mr. Jones was a principal person who chose the dignity principle. While I can't be sure of the exact role it has played in my life, I know it is one link in the chain that forms, holds, and shapes dignity for me.

And that is how dignity wins—one link at a time.

CHAPTER 3

The Dignity Gap
The Lack of Dignity and the Rise of Objectification

JEFF COULDN'T TAKE IT anymore. His frustration with Dave boiled over. He turned and yelled at the top of his lungs, "You are such an idiot!" and followed his outburst with a violent shove to Dave's chest. Dave responded with a step back, followed by a quick drop to his fighting stance and a tackle that left both men scrambling on the factory floor. Others quickly pulled them apart, hair disheveled, shirts torn, faces red, and their dignity violated.

Both men were brought before the floor manager Ed. Ed discovered this altercation had been brewing for some time. Jeff and Dave had been going back and forth with one another over workplace differences for months. Their shift manager had moved up the ladder and left a gap they both tried to fill. Each had a different opinion about how things should run. Jeff preferred the way the previous shift manager handled things. He was deliberate, focused, and efficient, and he flourished under his systems. Dave disliked the last shift manager and thought the leadership vacuum provided a way to bring some much-needed change to his work environment. He longed for a more transparent and cooperative environment. The two men discussed their thoughts at breaks and on occasion over lunch. They frequently talked with other employees, garnering what they believed to be popular support for their positions.

Soon the differences were not merely differences of opinion. They became personal. It wasn't just that they disagreed with one another; it was that the other person was the problem. They made derogatory comments under their breath whenever the other spoke in meetings. They called each other names when just out of earshot.

A work party provided another opportunity for escalation. Work parties tend to create different environments as work is not the focus when employees gather, and that's what happened here. The party was at a brewery that featured local brews and games like ping-pong, cornhole, and shuffleboard for the patrons to play. Teams formed, and competition commenced. Jeff and Dave were on opposite teams. Each cheered when the other missed the mark, and as the alcohol flowed, the tension ratcheted up. Dave's team won a hotly contested shuffleboard match, and the gloating began. Dave finally felt like he had one over on Jeff, and he let him know it. The beer helped.

"You guys suck!" he said with a laugh.

Jeff responded, "Screw you. You only won because you cheated. You're a cheater, just like you cut corners at work."

"What is that supposed to mean?" Dave asked.

"You know what I mean," Jeff replied.

At this, the others playing surrounded the men, leading them off in different directions, distracting them with other games and more beer.

Online they were "friends." Jeff used Facebook to post about family and occasionally something inspirational. Dave used it to voice his opinions about life and other matters. Jeff saw Dave's feed and sometimes commented a dissenting point of view but soon found the "rhetoric" too much to take. Each time he saw a post from Dave, he felt the tension build in his neck and shoulders, and he quickly scrolled past the latest meme so he didn't get upset. Eventually, he unfollowed him.

The Tiniest Hijacker

This story is not a stretch. Yuki Noguchi wrote about a similar encounter in a shirt factory in which an order for Trump shirts led to a "skirmish" on the factory floor.[12] As much as we may want to prevent it, people's lives come to the workplace.

The old idea about not bringing our personal lives to work is just that, old. We bring all of who we are into every place we go. We can't pretend that isn't true anymore. But problems come with acknowledging this truth. Not just that we have much more to take into account with one another on any given day, but that the lines between who we are at work, home, and other arenas are blurry. In short, we leak. Our "personal" lives seep into our "professional"

---

12 – Yuki Noguchi. "I Can't Work With You! How Political Fights Leave Workplaces Divided." NPR. https://www.npr.org/2020/01/28/798593323/i-cant-work-with-you-how-political-fights-leave-workplaces-divided (accessed March 8, 2022).

lives. Occasionally, there is a glimpse, a crack in the edifice that shows us what people are *really* like. We are much more than our jobs. We are much more than what we get paid to do.

> People are a surprising and profound mixture of their upbringing, experiences, joys, and pains. You can't judge a book by its cover.

It reminds me of a guy in my master's program. This guy was as strait-laced as one could imagine. He carefully combed his black hair to the side. His pants, even his jeans, were neatly creased and ironed perfectly. His shirts, always in proper order, were buttoned to the top, showing little to no neck. His shoes and belts always matched. The books he carried were neatly in order with no papers sticking out around the edges. He was always on time and ready to go. In every way, one would think this guy was as rigid as they come.

One day though, the neck of his shirt opened slightly, exposing what was underneath. And it was utterly shocking. There under his shirt was a crude necklace, made of some earthy material with shells and, as I remember, claws of some kind.

When I asked him about it, he told me about his upbringing. He grew up in a mountainous jungle region with little creature comforts. His neighbors who lived on the surrounding hills were former cannibals. It wasn't uncommon for him to go shirtless and shoeless, and the necklace reminded him of where he grew up. It was a big part of who he is.

Perhaps someone's sleeve pulls up slightly on a dress shirt revealing a tattoo, or someone climbs into a vehicle you hadn't envisioned them driving. Maybe a coworker comes into the office with a black eye; her professional attire and demure personality never indicated that she practices Brazilian Jiu-Jitsu and could choke you in a million different ways. People are a surprising and profound mixture of their upbringing, experiences, joys, and pains. You can't judge a book by its cover.

Appearances are not often what they seem to be; as such we often draw unfair conclusions about one another. We make each other out to be the enemy. We create biases in our mind. As I sit in the coffee shop writing this chapter, there is a young man with olive skin next to me. He is watching a video on his tablet that includes Arabic script and Muslim religious leaders speaking. Should I be concerned, or is he simply listening to a sermon that helps him live out a generous life of faith?

Everyone, including our coworkers, leak their fears and worries. They spill, drip, and drain from us as we go about our daily lives. We are worried about our safety, our future, our health, and our loved ones just to name a few. When it comes to others, we are worried people don't have our best interests in mind and may be trying to gain an advantage or may take advantage of us. These fears and worries give us every opportunity to jump to conclusions. When we do, we look to confirm our biases once again. We leave work, tell our stories about what a jerk Jeff is or what an idiot Dave is, and firm up our biases with those we chat with. We seek out people who will listen and agree with us. In their empathy, our friends and family unknowingly cement the idea a little deeper in our minds. We get reinforced in our beliefs about how right we think we are.

In the illustration of Jeff and Dave, their dislike of one another boiled over into a physical altercation. While most of us don't reach that point physically, we do reach it mentally in our minds and hearts. We fight with others in our minds. We have negative thoughts about those we don't like or we disagree with, and we confirm those thoughts repeatedly. We bounce them off our friends, family, and coworkers to gain confirmation. We look for endorsement of our ideas, and when we have them, we drive them deep. Ever heard someone say, "That's just the way they are, and nothing is going to change my mind about it?" We all do this.[13]

* * *

Once a thought takes root, it is just a short journey to action. When Jeff began to draw conclusions about Dave, he began to withdraw. In the break room, he sat outside hearing range from Dave. He sought out assignments that didn't involve interaction with Dave. For Dave's part, his assumption that Jeff was too tight-laced caused him to withdraw as well. He believed it was better to stay away

---

13 – Ben Yagoda, "The Cognitive Biases Tricking Your Brain," The Atlantic, September 2018, https://www.theatlantic.com/magazine/archive/2018/09/cognitive-bias/565775.

from Jeff than to cause any conflict. He sensed Jeff's disapproval and did everything he could to stay as far away as possible.

The brain is hardwired for this kind of behavior. Humans are experts at danger analysis, as described previously with my fainting goat episode. In more clinical analysis, Daniel Goleman, noted psychologist and author of *Emotional Intelligence*, coined the term "amygdala hijack." He says,

> When we're stressed, the part of the brain that takes over, the part that reacts the most, is the circuitry that was originally designed to manage threats—especially circuits that center on the amygdala, which is in the emotional centers of the brain. The amygdala is the trigger point for the fight, flight, or freeze response. When these circuits perceive a threat, they flood the body with stress hormones that do several things to prepare us for an emergency. Blood shunts away from the organs to the limbs; that's the fight or flee. But the response is also cognitive—and, in modern life, this is what matters most, it makes some shifts in how the mind functions. Attention tends to fixate on the thing that is bothering us, that's stressing us, that we're worried about, that's upsetting, frustrating, or angering us. That means that we don't have as much attentional capacity left for whatever it is we're supposed to be doing or want to be doing. In addition, our memory reshuffles its hierarchy so that what's most relevant to the perceived threat is what comes to mind most

easily—and what's deemed irrelevant is harder to bring to mind. That, again, makes it more difficult to get things done than we might want. Plus, we tend to fall back on over-learned responses, which are responses learned early in life—which can lead us to do or say things that we regret later. It is important to understand that the impulses that come to us when we're under stress—particularly if we get hijacked by it—are likely to lead us astray.[14]

The very thing designed to help can cause us to make significant errors in judgment. Given our current climate—politically, socially, and even professionally—it should not be surprising to learn that many of us are walking around with some level of amygdala hyperactivity. We may not all be time bombs waiting to go off in some public display, but a large enough percentage of us have been party to outbursts that defied logic. This isn't somehow corralled when we arrive at work. It could even be that work is the place that causes more stress and more amygdala activity.

The Fastest Climb

Hijacked, we focus on our greatest threat or our greatest fear and leave important tasks incomplete and relationships untended. Have you ever been so stressed you forgot something? It's easy to do, isn't it? Our thoughts lead to actions.

The Ladder of Inference describes how our thoughts lead to actions and how the movement happens in split seconds without us even realizing it.

---

[14] – "The Brain and Emotional Intelligence: An Interview with Daniel Goleman," Tricycle: The Buddhist Review, May 18, 2011, https://tricycle.org/trikedaily/brain-and-emotional-intelligence-interview-daniel-goleman.

Ladder of Inference

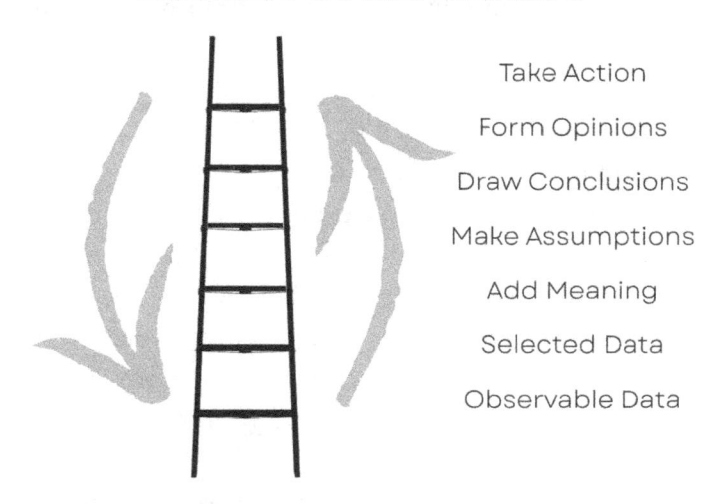

Take Action

Form Opinions

Draw Conclusions

Make Assumptions

Add Meaning

Selected Data

Observable Data

For example, during a speaking engagement, I took the time to meet many who were coming in. I noticed one man who quickly passed me, indifferent to my presence, while looking at his cell phone. He continued to look at his phone during my talk. He shifted in his seat and sighed audibly. When he yawned, he stretched his arms out his arms wide, almost as wide as he opened his mouth. Others noticed his behavior and were clearly distracted. His occasional glances up from his phone were just to survey the room, whereupon he quickly returned his attention to his device.

It was easy for me to draw conclusions. My inner monologue sounded like this: "He obviously got nothing from my talk, which is too bad because this guy could have used the information. He's like so many I've noticed before. They attend these talks or workshops, don't engage, and then give you terrible reviews with little feedback. These types are just jerks. They don't care about anyone but themselves and contribute little to society. I am definitely not going out of my way to chat with this guy when I finish. If he has a question, I'm not going to take it."

And all of this happened in seconds!

Sound familiar? Ever done that?

We build a case around a person without checking our thoughts and perceptions, which can lead us to draw incomplete and inaccurate conclusions:

- I start with observable data: a man walking swiftly, staring at his phone, bypassing me.
- I gather only selected data: his yawning and distracting behavior.
- I add my own meaning to what I see: I decide this guy doesn't want to be here.
- I make assumptions: He is bored and couldn't care less about being here.
- I draw conclusions: He thinks I am stupid and my topic is unimportant.
- I form beliefs: People like him are not worth my time and they distract those who are.
- I take action: I refuse to take a question or help him in any way.

All of this happens between my ears and without any question to its validity.

We move up and down the Ladder of Inference all the time, without anyone knowing it. What's worse, we can get stuck in a loop of thoughts that simply just reinforces our beliefs, so the next time I see this guy, or someone like him, I will select only data that supports what I already believe about him or people like him. To make matters worse, he has a Ladder of Inference as well. He watches me, selects data, adds meaning, makes assumptions, draws conclusions, forms beliefs, and takes actions. Before either of us know it, we have made objects out of one another.

In reality, he might have been distracted during my talk; maybe he was texting his wife about their terminally ill child. He might have been looking around the room to see if others were bored, or perhaps he was looking to see if a friend had arrived yet. He might have been bored, or he was just exhausted because he stayed up all night, consoling his sick child.

It's nearly impossible to know what is going on with someone short of stopping them and asking. This happens with individuals and groups. Imagine what would happen if groups moving up the Ladder of Inference got together—you would have a mob in no time, and it would be a veritable Ladder fest!

Think about this in your next work meeting or at a family gathering. There is so much more happening in these people than we know. And we can't know unless we engage with dignity.

This isn't always negative. We can have positive thoughts that lead to positive actions. For example, our thoughts of love for our spouses cause us to do any number of lovely and positive things. Picking up our socks, doing the dishes, or writing a little love note are all ways we do things based on our thoughts. When writing an evaluation or determining a bonus for a coworker, we think about what they've done, how they act, the value they add to the team, and share our praise with superiors.

That may seem obvious, but the negative is a bit more insidious and therefore all the more important to talk about and challenge.

Our repeated thoughts lead to repetition in our actions, and our actions become practice. On a good day, this looks like calculated caring for one another. On a bad day, it means we justify our poor behavior, which leads to the dangerous growth of a tiny germ in our minds to overgrown weeds of toxicity.

We don't have to look too far in the rearview mirror to see what this looks like. The scandals involving universities and religious institutions in which behavior was tolerated, overlooked, or covered up, have impacted thousands of innocent people and, by extension, their families and friends.

The final and most repulsive form of this is war and genocide. Perhaps you think I'm overreaching here. "Come on. It isn't that bad," you think, to which I ask, "Where does all the hatred and violence begin?" It begins in the heart and the mind, so attempting to deal with it before it becomes action or practice is critical.

If we can learn to think of one another differently, if we can learn to treat one another with dignity, we can change the course of our lives and the course of many others' lives. As Nelson Mandela said, "No one is born hating another person because of the color of his skin, or background or his religion. People must learn to hate, and if they can learn to hate, they can be taught to love, for love comes more naturally to the human heart than its opposite."[15]

---

15 – Nelson Mandela, *Long Walk to Freedom* (Back Bay Books, 1995).

Conclusion

Our culture and, by extension, our workplaces are majoring in *objectification*. Everyone is an "other" unless they are just like you. We are polarized and embittered, quick to point fingers and full of contempt. There is a major dignity disconnect happening, and it has found its way into every facet of our lives. No place is immune.

With objectification on the rise and division in our personal and work lives, it is not surprising that people feel increasingly isolated. Despite all our advances in technology and our ability to "connect" with information and one another, we are lonelier than ever. If we want to find out about people and what matters to them, we only need to Google them or look on social media. Instead of getting to know them over time and over coffee, we don our detective hats and research. But when we find in our research something with which we disagree on with the other, we magnify it (Inference Ladder!) and decide that, despite all we may have in common with that person, those one or two differences we have will surely make it impossible to connect, leaving us alone or isolated.

Is there any good news in all of this? Is there anything here in objectification, division, and our perceptions that can produce hope? Is there any way to overcome all that our culture promotes in these areas?

The simple answer is yes. We have a unique opportunity to significantly impact our homes, workplaces, and places in between. Dignity is like a light that shines in the dark in stark contrast to what's around it. Principled people unleashing the power of dignity can make an enormous difference.

Take a moment to think of those you regularly interact with. Each of them are dealing with the issues discussed in this chapter, and you have the opportunity to lean in and paint a different picture—one of dignity, one that communicates that people matter, not just for a bottom line, but because they exist. This heads off workplace conflict. Dignity keeps people like Dave and Jeff from grappling on the floor of the factory, and it can help you in every area of your life. Dignity is mission critical.

Companies and organizations are working hard to do this. Larger companies now have positions with titles like VP of Inclusion and Diversity with the goal of making sure the workplace looks like the rest of society—a mix of folks, not just one group. Inclusion and diversity are efforts to ensure that everyone, especially the marginalized, has a voice. That's the topic of the next chapter.

CHAPTER 4

Unleashing the Power

Closing the Gaps of Diversity and Inclusion

I REMEMBER MY SCHOOL DANCES well. The quintessential experiences for prepubescent tweens to commiserate over later in life. Come back with me if you dare.

The excitement builds knowing you will be in the room with your friends and those you might be attracted to or those who may be attracted to you. It starts with all the talking about the dance. What is the theme? Who is going? Who is going with whom? How will you get there? What will you do before and after? What will you wear?

My own experience is well in the past, but I recently relived these awkward moments through my children's eyes....

I was that parent who volunteered to chaperone the junior high school dance.

There were decorations. Balloons and streamers everywhere. The balloons were kicked around casually as people danced or by the overzealous young man who imagined them to be soccer balls and that he was in the World Cup, not at school dance (who wants to be at a dance anyway?). Occasionally there was a loud "pop" followed by the startled responses of the unprepared youngsters. The pieces of balloons rolled up on the floor or somehow found their way into the mouth of a soccer-playing young man.

The streamers on the wall, the ceiling, the tables were carefully twisted and taped for effect. Hours went into putting them in place only to have the humidity of warm-blooded youngsters cause the tape to loosen. The streamers became headbands, wristbands, or some weird version of a feather boa.

The music was always too loud, and the dancers leaned in to have conversations. Frequently, the talks occurred in the restrooms…and they happened in packs…particularly with the girls. They streamed out of the bathroom with newfound confidence, smiles, and giggles, having decided what to do about whatever situation they faced.

It was not uncommon to see a massive gap in the room. The few brave souls who ventured out on the floor were greeted with high-fives and smiles as the music ended, and they retreated back to their friend groups like some triumphant hero of days gone by. There was nearly always a clear dividing line—boys on one side, girls on the other—and a ton of nerves in the middle.

Dances are fraught with peril. The opportunity for embarrassment runs highs. Especially when asking someone to dance. It took a ton of courage for me to go to a dance, let alone asking someone to dance with me! Those horrible moments of walking across that massive gap, the distance between the boys and girls amplified by the lack of bodies on the dance floor, creating a forever space that must be crossed in order to connect with someone. All eyes on both sides were on me as I approached that girl (and her friend group) to ask if she would like to dance. My stomach churned as I waited for her response because it meant so much.

Will it be a yes or a no? Maybe later? An excuse? The totality of one's junior high existence depends on moments like these! What a terrible embarrassment to hear a rejection in whatever form it came—disgust, a laugh, or indifference. No matter how it happened, everyone could see it happened. The walk of shame back across the dance floor chasm to attempt to salvage one's ego was lonely and painful.

The Dignity Dance

Maybe you never attended a junior high dance. Or maybe yours were better than my experience as a student or my observation as an adult. Still, you're likely familiar with the feelings these situations produce: Will I get to go? Will I be left out? Do I matter?

Some have equated diversity as getting asked *to the dance*. For some time, only certain people have been invited to the dance, meaning only one type of person was allowed in the room in specific segments of organizations. But today, the goal *is* diversity. It has become clear that a variety of voices with various experiences gives companies and organizations a much better foundation to serve their employees and customers.

There is no "one size fits all" approach because there isn't "one," but many. The more diversity we have in our experiences and our lives, the better our ability to develop as people and learn from one another. Look around and ask these questions: *"Does everyone here look like me? Are they the same age, gender, socio-economic type, or skin color? Do they think differently from me?"* We easily create echo chambers; even well-intentioned people and leaders do it. The push for diversity is a worthwhile effort to make sure everyone gets to come to the dance.

No one likes to be left out. "When people are comfortable and can express themselves in an authentic way, they are more likely to perform better, which increases engagement and contributes to the organization as a whole," said Miguel Castro, senior director and lead for the Diverse Ecosystem, Global Diversity & Inclusion Office at SAP.[16]

We are in danger of sending the wrong message to potential hires. People ask the question if they want to work with and for you. They ask, "Do I want to work in a place dominated by one race, sex, or socio-economic group? Am I a good fit for a place that doesn't share my value of diversity?" When workplaces look monochromatic, it leaves out anyone who might appear different despite what they have to offer. Diversity means a seat at the table for anyone who can do the work regardless of appearance.

Inclusion, then, is getting asked *to dance*. If diversity is attending the dance, inclusion is getting on the dance floor. The folks at the table, in the meeting, or at crucial positions in the organization fully contribute and shape the environment or the culture of the space. Inclusion is not a box to be checked; it is critical in valuing others different from us. Not allowing others to have influence or participate makes

---

16 – Nicole Fallon, "How to Create an Inclusive Workplace Culture," Business News Daily, accessed November 12, 2022, https://www.businessnewsdaily.com/10055-create-inclusive-workplace-culture.html.

no sense. The reason we have diversity is for inclusion. We need the perspective of people who are different from us possess. While they cannot speak for an entire group, they can share their experiences and perspectives, which help inform and transform workplaces.

There is no point in diversity without inclusion. Getting asked to the big dance and not actually getting to dance sucks.

I'm reminded of "Night To Shine." Each year, on the Friday before Valentine's Day, a gala is held. Families with special needs students have the chance to celebrate together with their kids. Students who would not have the opportunity to attend a dance get the opportunity to not only go but to celebrate and dance with others, validating their worth while having a great time. Inclusion's purpose isn't just to get the right people to the dance but also for them to participate and play a role where they may have been unwelcome previously.

Getting on the dance floor makes a difference, but it doesn't achieve the most important thing.

Go back to the junior high dance. You witnessed it. You saw a friend stuck dancing with someone who didn't want to dance with them. Like two Frankenstein's monsters, they rigidly turned in circles as they avoided eye contact, and as soon as the song ended, they quickly split and go opposite ways. They might as well have been dancing with a mannequin. There was no joy, no expression, no meaning; they were just going through the motions.

Diversity and inclusion can become like that, just going through the motions. They can be boxes that organizations check rather than a way to value employees and customers.

Do we have the right people at the table? Check. Have they shared their ideas and opinions? Check. Have they contributed? Check. It may look great on a website or social media, but the practice of both is missing. Diversity and inclusion are like getting eighty meters into a 100-meter race. They are essential, even critical, but they don't get you where you want to go.

Because, to restate a critical point, *how* we do what we do is as important as *what* we do. You can check all the right boxes, you can say all the right things, and you can follow all the rules but still miss the mark. It's like treating the symptoms and not the cause.

Dignity is the missing piece to diversity and inclusion. Both diversity and inclusion are the *what*. Dignity provides the *how*. Having the right people in the room and participating in the meetings is one thing. Treating them with inherent value and honoring their dignity is quite another.

The goal of diversity and inclusion is related to critical pieces of business like providing safe spaces for employees, creating goodwill within and outside your organization, and helping drive profits and benefit the bottom line. One thing that is as true today as it has ever been: happy employees make good companies.

Millennials, the largest group in the workforce, are no different from those who've come before when it comes to wanting great jobs. However, they are looking for something very different. Now more than ever, people are asking: "What is it like to work there?" Of course, potential employees want to know about health benefits, salary, and perks, but more than that, they want to know they will be treated like a human being, not just a cog in the machine.

According to a Gallup Poll,[17]
- Millennials change jobs more often than do those of any older generation, and six in ten say they are currently looking for new employment opportunities.
- Millennials are less engaged in the workplace than are their older counterparts, and they are more likely to be categorized as "not engaged."
- Millennials' lack of engagement costs the U.S. economy hundreds of billions of dollars annually in lost productivity.
- Opportunities to learn and grow at work are highly important to Millennials when seeking out new jobs or deciding to stay in current ones.
- Millennials want to talk with their managers—and not always just about work. However, they are less comfortable approaching their managers to talk than their older counterparts are.

It sounds like dignity is at the heart of what this group is looking for. Providing a context for relationships and meaningful work that develops and grows and keeps them engaged is essential for this group. Keeping Millennials at work requires the same diligence as attracting them. Why would anyone want to work with you? Why would anyone want to work for you? Validating the dignity of those in your charge makes employees feel like real people and

---

17 – "How Millennials Want to Work and Live," Gallup.com, August 1, 2018, http://www.gallup.com/workplace/238073/millennials-work-live.aspx.

less like simple employees. They feel like they matter, and everyone wants to feel like they matter.

You are in business to make money or make the world a better place. You are about a bottom line. What is the point of a business or organization full of dignity that can't exist because it doesn't meet the critical goals (primarily financial) that it needs to meet? Friendly people don't add up to paychecks. But look at it this way: How you treat your employees matters, and the experience they have working with and for you, and the relationships and encouragement they receive matters.

Consider the Industrial Revolution. Dangerous machinery, massive metal wheels, and other industrial mechanisms stood under giant buildings with children attempting to work with them. There was little concern for the worker because they were simply a piece of the machinery. If one "broke," the company quickly replaced them. Fourteen-hour workdays were typical. Organizations gave little concern for the impact these factories might be having on the environment. The air and water quality diminished while they functioned with impunity.

Ironically enough, many of the images available from those days are black and white (color photography was not readily available). When employers only look at the bottom line, there is no color in the workplace. No joy. No humanity. No nuance. The only thing that needs to happen is to keep the machinery working. The bottom line is all that matters.

In between a responsible workplace and the bottom line is dignity. When people feel valued and appreciated, they work better.

According to an article posted by Glassdoor, the link is clear: "Based on one recent estimate, each 1 percent increase in customer satisfaction is linked to 4.6 percent higher company market values. That translates into a predicted boost in company market valuations of 7.8 to 18.9 percent for each 1-star improvement in overall rating on Glassdoor—a potentially large financial boost from better customer satisfaction via an improvement in employee morale."[18]

At the end of the day, you can check all the boxes and still miss the mark. Dignity isn't a box to check or a marker to be recognized. It is part of a culture and an ethos that values employees *and* accomplishes goals. It is the *how* to our *what*, and without it, our organizations will never flourish because our people won't thrive. Dignity looks like valuing people for who they are, not just what they contribute. It allows us to separate people from behaviors and celebrate who they are. Instead of the stiff-legged, wooden monster dance, dignity is the unashamed dance of celebration, laughter, acceptance, and joy.

---

18 – "How Glassdoor Reviews Impact Customer Satisfaction - Glassdoor for Employers," US | Glassdoor for Employers, August 7, 2019, https://www.glassdoor.com/employers/blog/glassdoor-reviews-customer-satisfaction.

CHAPTER 5
Donna Hicks on Dignity
Dignity's Key Role in Healthy Work Environments

ANY CREDIBLE CONVERSATION ON dignity must involve Dr. Donna Hicks. In addition to her writing and research, she's worked in some of the most challenging regions in the world when it comes to conflict and negotiation, including the Middle East, Northern Ireland, and Colombia. This work included partnering with the likes of the British Broadcasting Network and Archbishop Desmond Tutu.

She's created a list of "Ten Essential Elements of Dignity" as well as "Ten Temptations We Face to Violate Dignity." You can find both these lists in her books *Dignity: Its Essential Role in Resolving Conflict* and *Leading with Dignity: How to Create a Culture that Brings Out the Best in People*.

Ten Essential Elements of Dignity[19]

To create workplaces that foster dignity and environments where people can flourish, the "Ten Essential Elements of Dignity" need to be present. Obviously, having all ten and hitting them out of the park is the goal, but it could be that you've never considered them. It might be that you've never thought of them or the impact they may have on your context. To make the discussion of dignity more practical, what follows are brief explanations of each element as Dr. Hicks describes them in her books (*italicized paragraphs*) with my expansions. The aim is that they will benefit you as you grapple with becoming a dignity champion and close the dignity gap.

It is a worthwhile endeavor to take each validation and consider them for a time. Ask yourself some key questions like,

- Where have I seen this?
- Where is this missing?
- What role can I play in validations?
- What can I do when I see a violation?

These are practical, daily, and substantial ways to elevate the role dignity plays in all our relationships. As you read them, you may see a gap that needs addressing. I would encourage you to do what you can to close those gaps and lean into your relationships in new ways.

---

19 – Donna Hicks Ph D, *Dignity: Its Essential Role in Resolving Conflict* (Yale University Press, 2013).

ACCEPTANCE OF IDENTITY
Approach people as neither inferior nor superior to you; give others the freedom to express their authentic selves without fear of being negatively judged; interact without prejudice or bias, accepting how race, religion, gender, class, sexual orientation, age, disability, etc. are at the core of their identities. Assume they have integrity.

Let's not assume this is easy. It requires effort on your part not to put people in boxes so that you know what to do with them or how to treat them. When you do that, you objectify them, and that is never a good thing. Never. People act out of what they believe and especially whom they believe themselves to be. You have the opportunity and privilege to validate their dignity in workplaces, around the home, in your neighborhoods, and in your places of worship. No matter where you encounter another human being, you have a beautiful opportunity to validate their dignity.

This is essential to working with others. But it is also essential to how we think of ourselves and accepting our own identity.

RECOGNITION

Validate others for their talents, hard work, thoughtfulness, and help; be generous with praise; give credit to others for their contributions, ideas, and experience.

Recognition is a critical component for anyone with influence. Especially in the job space, if you don't recognize people for their work, who they are, or how they contribute, they will quickly feel like they don't matter. You will begin the process of a hiring, onboarding, and losing time and money. It is far better to recognize people for who they are and how they contribute. An exciting approach to this is from Gary Chapman and Paul White in *The Five Languages of Appreciation in the Workplace*. They have taken their work on Love Languages and turned it toward the workplace in helpful ways. You could leave out the word "love" and just go with 'language.' Recognition is a language many understand and value.

ACKNOWLEDGMENT

Give people your full attention by listening, hearing, validating, and responding to their concerns and what they have been through.

Don't you love it when you sit down with someone, maybe for coffee or lunch or another meeting, and the first thing they do is pick up their phone? So annoying!

But what if they turn off the ringer or put it on silent? If they are aware, maybe they set it on the table, or even more self-aware put it face down on the table. Now that's a big deal! The phone is access to another world—a world where you do not reside. Acknowledgment requires being fully present, not just present to someone's physical presence, but to all of whom they are and what they are experiencing. When you are with someone, don't think about being anywhere else. People can smell disingenuousness.

INCLUSION

Make others feel that they belong at all levels of relationship (family, community, organization, nation).

You can ask someone a great question: "How can I include you in this?" and let them answer. It may be an invitation to a meeting, an email, or text, but in some way, letting them know you want them to be a part of what is going on is essential. Another question is, "Who else needs to be involved?" This isn't just for stakeholders; it creates an atmosphere where people feel as if they matter and they are important. Inviting them into formal and nonformal spaces is another way to do it. An invitation to a quick coffee run or a critical meeting can speak volumes.

SAFETY

Put people at ease at two levels: physically, where they feel free of bodily harm; and psychologically, where they feel free of concern about being shamed or humiliated, that they feel free to speak without fear of retribution.

Later in this book, we will talk about fear, but talking about it twice doesn't hurt. Fear is maybe the most powerful motivating factor people face. It causes you to do any number of illogical and "crazy" things. It can cause you to be silent when you need to speak and remain still when you need to act.

FAIRNESS

Treat people justly, with equality, and in an evenhanded way, according to agreed upon laws and rules.

A false balance is an abomination to the Lord, but a just weight is his delight. (Proverbs 11:1)

Ancient people knew the value of fairness, and not many things get employees and customers out of balance and disengaging than inequality in treatment. Once they see that people aren't playing by the established norms and that there is preferential treatment, it doesn't take them long to find the exit. However, when you treat people fairly and evenly, including ourselves, you win trust and confidence with others and earn their respect. This reinforces your integrity and helps people to see you are worth partnering with. This includes how you treat yourself. It is hard to respect people who treat others one way, but then treat themselves poorly.

INDEPENDENCE
Empower people to act on their own behalf so that they feel in control of their lives and experience a sense of hope and possibility.

Helping people take advantage of opportunities and encouraging them along the way creates an environment where risk is acceptable and outcomes, while important, aren't the only metric. The ability to entrust people with tasks and celebrate their accomplishments says as much about you as it does them. People flourish when they know they can, in some way, control what happens around them.

UNDERSTANDING
Believe that what others think matters; give them the chance to explain their perspectives, express their points of view; actively listen in order to understand them.

One of the ways to invalidate someone and their opinion is to tell them, "I know." "I know what you are going to say, I know what you think, I know you don't like this." It's presumptuous, you know? Even if you do know, preventing them from engaging with you by preempting their comments doesn't help. Asking good questions and avoiding the "why" question can go a long way toward understanding. The "why" question puts people in a defensive posture and assumes they must answer for what they've done. It doesn't engender relationships but forces a courtroom-like response. Trying to understand is a different way of getting to the data you need. Seeking context to decisions, including how they felt, puts a human element on any circumstance.

BENEFIT OF THE DOUBT
Treat people as trustworthy; start with the premise that others have good motives and are acting with integrity.

It's easy to formulate opinions about people and make conclusions about their motivations. Earlier, we discussed the Ladder of Inference. Giving people the benefit of the doubt keeps you from moving up the ladder too quickly. Your first response, not unlike fight or flight, is to ensure your safety, so you may approach people and relationships with caution and distrust. But when this is your posture, people might feel like they have to prove themselves to you in some vague way. This isn't blind trust on your part, but when dignity is validated, you have an open approach and you believe the best in those you work with and for. A question you can ask is: What is the most respectful interpretation (MRI) of their actions I can have? MRI is a helpful approach from the boardroom to the living room and validates dignity.

ACCOUNTABILITY

Take responsibility for your actions; if you have violated the dignity of another, apologize; make a commitment to change hurtful behaviors.

People (for the most part) learn at an early age that doing the wrong thing has consequences. Some of those are steep and painful; some are small and go largely unnoticed. When you foresee the results are something you don't want to face, you learn the art of deflection. This looks like making sure the blame goes to others, or at least others share the responsibility with you. You become good at lying, telling half-truths, and throwing people under the bus, all so that you can save face or avoid paying the price for your actions. Leaders who lead with integrity and dignity take responsibility for their actions. They don't blame, deflect, or redirect. They admit their mistakes, empathize with how they impacted those around them, apologize, and commit to change. Great leaders are transparent with their plan about how this change will happen and invite others to help them with the steps.

The Ten Temptations to Violate Dignity[20]

On the flip side, we can do some serious damage to our relationships with others when we violate their dignity. Whether it's co-workers or family, the way we interact with one another matters. We may unknowingly be violating the dignity of those around us. Dr. Hicks adds ways (again in *italics*) in which we are tempted to violate the dignity others possess along with my expansions on each one.

TAKING THE BAIT

Don't take the bait. Don't let the bad behavior of others determine your own. Restraint is the better part of dignity. Don't justify getting even. Do not do unto others as they do unto you if it will cause harm.

As silly as it seems, the worldview so many possess is that if someone does you harm, real or perceived, you get to pay them back, and your payback will be worse than the damage you received because you want to make sure it doesn't happen again. Remember Jeff and Dave? Are humans really this petty? The answer is yes. You are triggered, your amygdala goes into overdrive, and you respond. Keeping yourself at the bottom of the ladder is critical when you don't want to simply react to someone's bad behavior. When you are quick to listen and slow to anger, it allows you to stay in charge and not be governed by those around you so easily.

---

20 – Donna Hicks Ph D, *Leading with Dignity: How to Create a Culture That Brings Out the Best in People* (Yale University Press, 2018).

SAVING FACE

Don't succumb to the temptation to save face. Don't lie, cover-up, or deceive yourself. Tell the truth about what you have done.

Many temptations around dignity violations respond to fear. You are motivated to save face to avoid looking bad; you are literally trying to save the face of the image you put up for everyone to see. Unfortunately, when you do this, you engage in behaviors that are beneath you and lead to more behaviors that violate your own dignity.

SHIRKING RESPONSIBILITY

Don't shirk responsibility when you have violated the dignity of others. Admit it when you make a mistake and apologize if you hurt someone.

It's easy to blame someone else for what's happened. Our culture tends to celebrate it. There is always someone to point a finger and someone with their phone out to record behavior. Narratives follow these things quickly, painting pictures of incidents that may or may not be accurate. It feels at times that this is the major use of social media. This temptation runs deep, though it is easy and surface level. So when it comes to your behavior, you must own your actions. There is a saying that attempts to cover this temptation: "We judge others by their actions, but we judge ourselves by our motivations."

> **SEEKING FALSE DIGNITY**
> *Beware of the desire for external recognition in the form of approval and praise. If we depend on others alone for validation of our worth, we are seeking false dignity. Authentic dignity resides within us. Don't be lured by false dignity.*

This is a challenging temptation in a world of feedback and reward. You may be tempted to assume that your worth is caught up in what you do, not only that but in how well you do what you do. When you succumb to this temptation, you are only as good as your last performance or how impressive your title is, or how people may feel about you (at that moment). However, your situation can change quickly, and so can the opinion of others. For example, many football coaches are fired a couple seasons after being named Coach of the Year. Add Salesperson, Teacher, Employee of the Year, etc., and you get the meaning. Your dignity is found in *who you are*, not your job or in people's opinions.

> **SEEKING FALSE SECURITY**
> *Don't let your need for connection compromise your dignity. If we remain in a relationship in which our dignity is routinely violated, our desire for connection has outweighed our need to maintain our own dignity. Resist the temptation to settle for false security.*

I can't count how many times I've sat with people who are in dignity-violating relationships. It might be with a spouse, significant other, or a job. The temptation to feel secure is a natural and vital need, but not at the expense of your dignity. Abusive relationships at work or home are unfortunately common. Your need to connect, feel loved, appreciated, and valued is so great that you are tempted to forgo the primary place of dignity to embrace something far short.

AVOIDING CONFLICT

Stand up for yourself. Don't avoid confrontation when your dignity is violated. Take action. A violation is a signal that something in a relationship needs to change.

Conflict is not a bad thing. A little louder for the people in the back: *Conflict is not a bad thing.* We often avoid it because we don't want to "rock the boat" or "it isn't worth it." When you say these things, you are talking about the other person's boat and you are deciding your relationship with that person isn't significant enough to risk more injury. The problem here is that the boat getting rocked is *yours*, and you *are* worth it. It's not about them. Finding courage in accepting your dignity is a key to avoiding this temptation.

> **BEING THE VICTIM**
> *Don't assume that you are the innocent victim in a troubled relationship. Open yourself to the idea that you might be contributing to the problem. We need to look at ourselves as others see us.*

The ability to reflect on a situation and a relationship is critical. Choosing victimhood is an easy way out of a problem or a relationship. It's simple to paint someone in a terrible light in your mind or with your words. Conversely, it's just as simple to paint yourself in an angelic light, without flaws. A meaningful way to avoid this temptation is to ask yourself and a trusted advisor: What are some ways I've contributed to this problem? Getting some perspective can make this temptation easier to avoid.

> **RESISTING FEEDBACK**
> *Don't resist feedback from others. We often don't know what we don't know. We all have blind spots; we all unconsciously behave in undignified ways. We need to overcome our self-protective instincts and accept constructive criticism. Feedback gives us an opportunity to grow.*

When you ask good questions from yourself and from others, you may get data you don't like. You may find you aren't as great as you think, and perhaps those you are in a relationship with aren't as bad as you believe them to be. There's an old saying, "Wounds from a friend are faithful." A well-timed and pointed conversation with someone who knows you well can help immensely. Resisting what people say because you are afraid it might be true or hurt will only keep you from being healthy and embracing your dignity.

BLAMING AND SHAMING OTHERS TO DEFLECT YOUR OWN GUILT

Don't blame and shame others to deflect your own guilt. Control the urge to defend yourself by making others look bad.

As Brene Brown points out in her Ted Talk, "Listening to Shame," shame and guilt aren't the same things. Shame is "I am bad." Guilt is "I did something bad." Shame is based on identity; guilt is based on behavior. When you make mistakes, you want to argue that it isn't as bad as another person: "At least I'm not like Helen." The more distance you put between your shame and guilt, the better you feel. However, dragging others down to make yourself look better only lowers the bar for everyone. No one wins.

> **ENGAGING IN FALSE INTIMACY AND DEMEANING GOSSIP**
>
> *Beware of the tendency to connect by gossiping about others in a demeaning way. Being critical and judgmental about others when they are not present is harmful and undignified. If you want to create intimacy with another, speak the truth about yourself, about what is happening in your inner world, and invite the other person to do the same.*

Reputation destruction and gossip are powerful tools when you feel powerless or when you want to manipulate. But they are undignified in every way. When you ask the question, "Would I say this if they were here?" is a helpful way to avoid picking up these tools. Another way to think about it is: "Am I connecting with who is in front of me based on the behavior of someone who isn't?" Gossip and reputation destruction are harmful to dignity, but not only to those you gossip about but also harm you when you do it.

* * *

It's easy to violate another's dignity. The temptations are everywhere. Sometimes it feels like it's too much work to validate others. When we choose the easy, and dare I say, lazy way of violation, we continue the vicious cycle in which we are currently stuck. It takes intention and work to move past the cheap ways of being together towards a more robust humanity. Only such strong and meaningful work as this will help us become dignity champions and that work is for us to do. We can't rely on someone else to do it.

Now that you know, you are accountable. The power you possess is unmeasurable. You may feel frail and unable as you look in the mirror, but you are worthy. You know how many times you've chosen the weak, pale version of human interaction. We've all done it. Deciding to be different doesn't mean we're perfect or that our past is free from flaws. Far from it. What it does mean is that when we make mistakes, we deal with it in a dignified way.

Next, we will look at what to do when you blow it and how you can stay on the path of dignity.

CHAPTER 6
The Surprising Place of Dignity
What to Do When You Blow It

IT DOESN'T TAKE LONG to realize the world is not a perfect place. We see and experience things that let us know life is hard, and things don't always go the way we think they should.

If we were honest, we would admit we're part of the problem.

But then again, it's really easy to say, "No one's perfect."

While that's true, it does not excuse us from poor behavior. Worse yet, saying "no one's perfect" is little help to those who are hurting or to those we need to address about something we've done. That kind of "apology" causes more damage than it does soothe relationships.

We all blow it from time to time, but the power of dignity is experienced and manifested when we address our mistakes well.

I was recently the unfortunate recipient of oral surgery. I didn't do my homework to ask how long recovery was, what I should expect, and how best to manage postoperative pain.

After the procedure, it was not long before the numbness wore off and the pain kicked in. And the pain was blinding. I took the medications, iced my face, and did some form of primitive dance to stop the pain. None of it worked.

After a few days of dancing, medication, ice, and terrible grumpiness, I called the office to see what I could do. When they kindly scheduled me for a visit (squeezing me in when I had no appointment), I was fit to be tied and less than happy.

The receptionist and the dental assistant were kind, despite my dark demeanor and short answers to their questions. When the dentist came in, I asked her what was going on and why I was in so much pain. She assured me it was to be expected and gave me a different prescription. They treated me with kindness and empathy, which I didn't return.

I blew it.

I was curt and unfriendly and dismissive.

I could easily say I was in pain. I could argue my way around why I behaved the way I did, and all that is well and good. But the truth is, I did not treat them with dignity. I violated their dignity because I was in pain.

It was important to realize the ways in which I violated their dignity beyond just admitting that I was a jerk. To take this seriously I looked at the ten temptations (from the last chapter). Specifically, I was a victim, they were the problem, and I blamed others for something I could have done to limit the problem. (If this resonates with you, take a look at those temptations again, and see where you are prone to go.)

The next several days weren't easy. The medication helped, but it was a rough ride. After a week, I was back on track and doing much better. I apologized to my wife and kids for being so grouchy and unhelpful, but I know there was another stop to make. I knew I needed to offer another apology at the dentist's office. I had to apologize for my behavior. Fortunately, I had an upcoming appointment that would give me the opportunity.

As I arrived, I apologized to the receptionist. It went something like this:

"Hi, I'm here for my appointment."

"Great! We've got you checked in."

"Do you have a moment?" I asked.

"Sure." The receptionist answered smiling, though maybe a bit unsure of what was about to happen.

"A few weeks ago, you fit me in when I had an emergency with my tooth. I am so thankful for you doing that."

"It was no problem. I was happy to help."

"Well, when I came in, I was in a lot of pain and behaved really poorly. I was short with you and didn't thank you for getting me in. You've always been kind and didn't deserve how I treated you. I am sorry."

She waved her hand in the air and said, "Oh, don't worry about it. It happens all the time, and I could see you were in a lot of pain. It is no big deal."

"What you did for me was a big deal and I am grateful," I responded, "and I wanted you to know how sorry I am that my actions didn't reflect it. Thanks for being so gracious."

"No worries; nothing to apologize for," she said smiling.

The interactions with the assistant and the dentist were similar. They were kind and forgiving and I was glad I had the chance to apologize.

Do all apologies go this way? No.

Do people always see the need to apologize? Most certainly not.

Can this create some uncomfortable moments? It sure can.

The power of dignity can overcome all of these and build stronger bonds between people and make relationships even better.

You can be sure it will take a lot for me to change dental providers now. I have more trust in them and confidence that even at my worst, they are willing to stay connected to me.

Taking this to thirty-thousand feet, how can this apply to our lives and dignity?

I put it into three steps.

Step One: Recognizing you blew it.

This can be difficult to grasp. Some people do not possess the internal compass that points them in the direction of relationships and seeing that they have made a mistake. It is hard to swallow. As a result, they might be unaware or uncaring of how they've impacted others. A great way to overcome this issue is to ask the question: How is my behavior impacting those around me?

Asking ourselves good questions is important. But a still better way of getting to the issue is to ask someone you trust that question. Get the information from someone else about how you come across or how you are perceived, especially when you think there is a problem or when someone has brought one to your attention. Clarity on intent and impact is critical (we will discuss both intent and impact more thoroughly later).

Step Two: Pause and reflect.
Once you know you've violated someone's dignity, it's important to pause and reflect. What specifically did you do? What were your behaviors and motivations? Grasping and knowing these things with our eyes and hearts open, we can ask which violations we engage in.

Being specific about our actions and about the way someone was treated is critical. It means that we take our role in the relational break seriously and that we take the other person and their thoughts and feelings seriously as well. It is helpful but not necessary to refer to the list of violations in chapter 4. The ability to say "I hurt you" is just as important.

Identifying the key pieces of the interaction(s) means we have the components of an apology.

Step Three: Apologize.
Amy Morin, author of *13 Things Mentally Strong People Don't Do* and host of the Verywell Mind Podcast, notes that there are three more things needed for your interaction.

Referring to the journal *Negotiation and Conflict Management Research*, she says you need sincerity, because your apology must be heartfelt, and you need to want to close the gap for the violation you caused.

If you are not sincere and heartfelt, the people you've hurt will not want to hear from you. Most people can smell insincerity from a mile away, which will only add insult to injury when you try to apologize even though you don't mean it or don't care. Your mom isn't making you do this; it must come from you and your own sense of empathy.

Morin lists the six components of a good apology as shared in the journal:
1. Expression of regret
2. Explanation of what went wrong
3. Acknowledgment of responsibility
4. Declaration of repentance
5. Offer of repair
6. Request for forgiveness

It is not terribly shocking to realize that many are unable or unwilling to walk down the road of apology. There is little for us to value in admitting we've created a gap in relationships or made a critical error. If we value integrity and relationships, apologizing is not always easy, but the benefits are great.

The journal states what feels obvious, if you are apologizing, you have a sense of regret. This isn't that simple though. People are sorry for a lot of things, but not always their behavior. Ever try to help a child apologize? They don't always regret what they've done. Adults are no different. They may not like what their actions produced, but it is always easy to say things like, "I am sorry you feel that way." Or, "I am sorry that happened to you." Which expresses no regret at all. A+B=C. What I did hurt you. I am sorry I hurt you.

In explaining what went wrong, we often try to explain away our actions. Remember how we judge others by their actions but ourselves by our motivations? This is especially true here. We don't isolate our mistakes but like to add words that justify our actions. It is better to say "I was wrong." Even when you think your motives were pure. We have to own it.

Taking responsibility for our behavior sounds a lot like a dignity validation, doesn't it? There is an important link between dignity and our humility. It is the oil that allows for lesser friction, even in the hardest conversations.

* * *

I like what the journal says about numbers five and six.

Offering to repair may or may not make sense given the circumstances but it means you take this seriously. Looking back on my interaction with the dentist's office, I could have offered to buy the office coffee, or simply come with coffee in hand, to help them see my level of remorse and desire to make our relationship right. It could be seen as trying to "buy off" my guilt, but coupled with a heartfelt attitude and the proper steps, it could have the opportunity to be received as desired. (Coffee is always a good way to express closeness in a relationship; I'll provide information where you can send some my way.)

Allowing someone to tell you how you can make amends is important. It puts the power back in their hands. Your willingness to follow through on what you say is critical. If they simply say "don't do it again," do everything in your power to follow through. If you don't, you will become untrustworthy, and your apologies will mean very little.

To elaborate further on number six, asking for forgiveness is hard. We are completely at the mercy of someone else. We can only receive. When I say mercy, I mean the withholding of a just punishment. Mercy is critical to being human. If all we ever do is treat people according to what they deserve, none of us would be very happy. I need mercy daily from those I love and those around me. We break rules, we are selfish, and we act poorly when hurt. Imagine a world in which no one forgives anything, in which no one overlooks an offense, in which no one is willing to have empathy or understanding for the complex ways humans behave. That is not a world I want to live in and certainly not a world of mercy and forgiveness.

Asking forgiveness means you understand what you've done and the problems it caused or the dignity it violated.

What Does It Mean to Forgive?

Forgiveness means you will not treat the person according to what their actions deserve. It means you will not hold their actions against them. It means when you think of them, you do not have bitterness in your heart. To be sure, forgiveness is a process. It doesn't mean you sweep things under the rug, but that you genuinely restore the relationship.

Asking this of someone is a big deal. Once someone gives it, treating it as precious and with great care is the only way forward. To trample one's forgiveness is to re-violate their dignity with perhaps even greater consequences.

We are happy to receive forgiveness but perhaps less likely to give it away. Consider this as you approach number six.

A good apology can be ointment to a wound. It can bring about humility and create room for compassion. While it may not always "work" the way you hope, it opens the door for healing and relationship down the road.

Practice apologizing for big and little things you've done. In doing so, you will find it isn't as bad as you think, and it validates dignity beautifully. In fact, blowing it and apologizing well can unleash the power of dignity to heal and create stronger bonds.

One of the reasons that we don't apologize or that we're content with how we've treated another person is fear. We fear being wrong, getting hurt again, looking bad, or a whole host of other fears. Fear is where we are in our culture and where we are with one another. Next, we look at fear and the role it plays in how we live together.

CHAPTER 7
The Role of Fear in Dignity
Why Facing Your Fear Matters

FEAR IS ONE OF the most important topics we can address when talking about dignity. Why? Because it's the unseen force behind nearly every interaction we have. It seeps into our minds and into our hearts, causing us to think and act in ways we don't realize.

Sometimes we are aware of the thing we fear and can face it head-on. However, oftentimes fear grips us in subtle ways that cause us to change how we think of ourselves and others to the point of erasing dignity from our relationships. That's why I love talking about fear at speaking engagements and with my clients.

All of us like the idea of reaching for our dreams. We love the stories about people who lived in such a terrible state but believed so much in their dreams they were able to pull themselves out of their situation. Those stories feel good and inspire us to be better people and dream that maybe we can do it, too.

While these feel-good stories are worthy of admiration and retelling, the story of fear points to a different motivation.

I grew up in Western Montana, in the woods near the rivers, trees, and wildlife. It's not that I was much of a woodsman or hunter, but I did grow up with a sense of connectedness to what was around me. Swimming in rivers, bonfires in the woods, and sleeping under the stars seemed normal.

Using common sense about how to behave in those activities was just that—common sense. Nearly everyone I knew understood how to keep the fishing rod tip up when a trout was on the line. Everyone knew that when they saw bear cubs they were in trouble because momma bear was close behind and she might not take kindly to anyone admiring her children. Or when a bison was nearby everyone kept their distance because those animals are big, cantankerous, and fast (as visitors to Yellowstone learn the hard way every year). That's how I grew up.

So when I found myself lost in the woods in the dead of winter, that was a problem.

Most years growing up, our family went into the woods to find our Christmas tree. It was a far-from-idyllic experience though. There was no hot cocoa and mittens, no snowball fights, and no roaring fire. It was all about driving an ill-equipped vehicle up a logging road while trying not to skid over into the abyss that lurked around every turn on the mountainside. Dad was adventurous, so getting a tree was something akin to an epic journey like *Lord of the*

Rings. We ventured far past suitable trees, past hills and meadows into the mountains where he was sure the best Christmas trees lived.

One year on one of these little adventures, deep in the heart of these mountains, I got turned around. We'd been out most of the day, doing something that I can't remember now, but I do remember a couple of feet of snow covered the ground as new snow kept falling. The gray sky slowly faded from light to twilight, and we still didn't have a tree.

A funny thing happens in the winter, in the woods, in the snow; it's quiet. Like real quiet. The kind of quiet that hurts your ears. The snow falls in silence, and your breath disappears in front of your face like a whisper. Sound just seems to stop. It leaves your lips and drops dead in front of you.

I had followed my dad, who had traipsed around various areas, by watching his footprints in the snow. We chatted a bit as we walked, but it wasn't uncommon for him to get a bit ahead of me in the twists and turns. As long as I could see his footprints, I was okay.

The snow had started to fall more seriously as I stopped to inspect a particular tree. What I hadn't observed was how, even in that deep snow, I was losing sight of his tracks. I walked around a small stand of Douglas fir, thinking I might have found perfection when I noticed my dad was nowhere in sight. Glancing at the tracks, I could see where I had been and the circle I made around the trees, but as I walked around and around, I couldn't see how I had gotten there.

How could I have been so dumb? I knew better than to let this happen.

I quickly called out to my dad, thinking he was surely within earshot. But my calls met no response. I thought about what direction we had come in but realized my head was down the whole time, watching the tracks and not paying attention to where I was. The funny thing about being in the woods is that all the trees look the same. I knew I was in trouble and felt fear creep in.

I knew the sting of the cold on the skin when frostbite was near. I heard stories of people freezing in the woods just a few yards from safety. The danger was real. I was tired, hungry, and wanted the safety of the car.

I began to walk in concentric circles, slowly widening my path and calling out for my dad. I tried to use reason while combating the growing feeling of fear that threatened to overtake me. I knew panicking would only make things worse, so I did all I could to stay calm.

Five Basic Fears

Reflecting on and thinking about fear and motivation, I now see things more clearly. My first question: Was I motivated by what I wanted, or was I motivated by what I didn't want?

> *What I wanted was to be safe.*
> *I wanted to be with my dad.*
> *I wanted to be warm.*
> *I wanted to have food and water.*
> *I wanted certainty of a good outcome.*
>
> *What I didn't want was to freeze.*
> *I didn't want to get lost.*

I didn't want to be alone.
I didn't want to die or lose digits because of the cold.
I didn't want to be eaten by a hungry critter.
I didn't want to continue in uncertainty about my future.

Which part of what I wanted or didn't want was more motivating? Was I motivated more by what I feared or by what I wanted? Were they really all that different?

In an article written for *Psychology Today*, Dr. Karl Albrecht describes five basic fears we all share. I quote them below.[21]

1. Extinction—the fear of annihilation, of ceasing to exist. This is a more fundamental way to express it than just "fear of death." The idea of *no longer being* arouses a *primary existential anxiety* in all normal humans. Consider that panicky feeling you get when you look over the edge of a high building.
2. Mutilation—the fear of losing any part of our precious bodily structure; the thought of having our body's boundaries invaded, or of losing the integrity of any organ, body part, or natural function. Anxiety about animals, such as bugs, spiders, snakes, and other creepy things arises from fear of mutilation.
3. Loss of Autonomy—the fear of being immobilized, paralyzed, restricted, enveloped, overwhelmed, entrapped, imprisoned,

---

21 – Karl Albrecht, "The (Only) 5 Fears We All Share," Psychology Today, March 22, 2012, http://www.psychologytoday.com/us/blog/brainsnacks/201203/the-only-5-fears-we-all-share.

smothered, or otherwise controlled by circumstances beyond our control. In physical form, it's commonly known as claustrophobia, but it also extends to our social interactions and relationships.
4. Separation—the fear of abandonment, rejection, and loss of connectedness; of *becoming a non-person*—not wanted, respected, or valued by anyone else. The "silent treatment," when imposed by a group, can have a devastating effect on its target.
5. Ego Death—the fear of humiliation, shame, or any other mechanism of profound self-disapproval that threatens the *loss of integrity of the self*; the fear of the shattering or disintegration of one's constructed sense of lovability, capability, and worthiness.

These fears cause us to act, react, or not act (which is a reaction), and nearly all of them are in play as we go about our daily routines.

When someone is lost in the woods in the wintertime, the most understandable fear is death or Extinction. The possibility increases as the temperature drops outside and inside the body. After that, losing one's fingers or toes and maybe part of the nose or ear due to the cold is a reality one must face; Albrecht describes this as fear of Mutilation. In my scenario, Loss of Autonomy and Ego Death were at play as well. For me, four out of five of the biggest common fears were active at that moment.

Let's consider your work world. What motivates you in your job? Is it the pay? And are you more motivated by the fear of not having money or by the things that money frees you to do? Not having a paycheck may equal the inability to pay rent or a mortgage, which puts you at risk of Loss of Autonomy and likely Ego Death. Maybe not having a salary causes you to miss out on buying that boat you've saved for or taking that trip you planned. Interestingly, that involves the Loss of Autonomy and perhaps Ego Death as well (though maybe it's more like FOMO, fear of missing out). Not having a job may mean not having insurance for you and your family. Without insurance, you could be subject to insurmountable medical bills or the inability to cover basic healthcare needs.

Diving Deeper into Fear

When we start to dissect this, we see how fear lies behind much of the daily human experience. While most of us aren't in life and death situations daily (unless our occupations put us there), we still face fears grounded in the five basic expressions we share.

Think of it this way:
- A fear of heights is a fear of Extinction, Mutilation, and possibly Loss of Autonomy.
- Likewise, a fear of spiders (which makes perfect sense), snakes, or other creatures that can harm is likely a fear grounded in Extinction and Mutilation.
- Fear of public speaking is likely grounded in fear of Loss of Autonomy, Separation, and Ego Death.

- Fear of the dark, drowning, or claustrophobia are likely linked to Loss of Autonomy, Extinction, and maybe Mutilation.

The ability to link our fears to what we're *really* afraid of helps us identify what is *actually* happening, not just what's happening between our ears and in our nervous system. There are many more fears we face every day that we may not realize are active. Perhaps you identify with some of these:

- Of being corrupted or corrupt: An example of this is turning into something you are not by the influence of others. The fear is that you would change in some way that you may or may not be aware of.
- Of being unlovable: I wish this was less common, but, unfortunately, somewhere along the line, people believe they are not lovable. This fear causes them to do almost anything to get the love they long for and possibly reject those who really love them.
- Of being worthless: If you think about the word "worthless," it literally means "worth less," but less than what is the question. With this fear, people are afraid they have zero value. They fear having nothing to add and will go a long way (often unhealthy ways) to keep this fear from being realized.
- Of having no impact or identity: Like other fears, people who orient to this idea will do much in their power to prove they are

important or leave their mark. But, instead of a positive approach, their lives are motivated to make sure they matter and prove others wrong.
- Of being useless, helpless, or incapable: Fear of powerlessness causes many to "power up." They do so in a meeting or at an odd time, dying on hills that make no sense, interrupting or inserting themselves in places that aren't necessary.
- Of being without support and guidance: Feeling lost and without help is a terrible experience. Our friends, neighbors, and co-workers will work very hard to ensure they don't realize this fear. They may overshare, look for input, or cling to people they believe will be with them in their challenges.
- Of being deprived and in pain: Pain avoidance can cause a lack of decision-making, risk-taking, or paralysis by analysis. While no one likes pain, fear of something that hasn't happened just because it could happen (newsflash, pain is a part of life) creates a dynamic that orients to the negative possibilities versus the good that could be.
- Of being harmed or controlled by others: Being fearful of people, their actions, and their motivations make trusting anyone incredibly difficult. Yet, it's impossible to build any meaningful relationship without trust, let alone any business or organization.
- Of loss and separation: Many of these types of fears will be realized. They aren't an "if" but a

"when." Loss is part of the human experience as we face any number of losses as we age and live with one another. They may be loss of identity, ability, relationships, or dreams. Living in fear of loss and separation keeps us from being fully present and robs us and others of the gifts we are to one another.

These fears operate in every person every day. Still, we go about our lives—raising children, working, eating and drinking, enjoying one another and our different experiences—largely unparalyzed by what may be motivating us along the way.

How does this connect to dignity?

Talking about fear and dignity is critical because they are both parts of being human. Both are in operation at any given moment and are likely in operation in ways we don't know or understand. Dignity is an inherent nobility that can't be bought, sold, lost, or stolen. It is what it means to be human. According to Albrecht, fear is "an anxious feeling caused by our anticipation of some imagined event or experience."[22] Everyone has fears, whether we admit it or not. Our brains are hardwired to see them and avoid them. The classic fight-or-flight response is part of this dynamic.

But why all this talk about fear? We need two things at work to help us move forward together: the preferred future that dignity offers and the future we would like to avoid.

What could happen if we began our relationships with dignity as the baseline? What benefits might we and others experience if treating one another with dignity and

---

22 – Ibid.

validating one another's dignity was normative behavior? How would our work environments change? What would our personal relationships look like? What kind of lives might our children lead if we practice the dignity principle?

Consider what's at stake if we choose not to move forward together with dignity. We will continue to lose people, income, and potential, and build environments filled with efforts that address symptoms and not causes at work. We will continue suffering dignity violations in our relationships because people are intentionally causing violations or because they are ignorant. We will continue down the road of polarization and othering, blaming everyone else but ourselves for the problems we face together or personally.

The stakes are real, and the cost is high. It's becoming more and more essential that we get to the bottom line of how we interact with one another.

That bottom line is dignity.

It is easy to fear what might happen if we decide to move forward with dignity. There is uncertainty about how people might react: What will they say? What will they think? How will the power dynamics change? The whole host of unknowns is a fear itself.

To unleash the power of dignity, we must face fear. It may be the fear of our environments or the fear that wells up inside us in the face of the unknown. Sometimes, facing our own fears is the more significant task.

Back to the woods...

I found my dad. Luckily, he heard my voice in my efforts to avoid freezing, and we found each other. He knew the way back to safety and we walked to the car together.

He pulled out the keys and fired up the engine, and soon I was filled with warmth and security.

Dignity knows the way through fear, uncertainty, and difficulty.

Dignity is just like that. It knows the way through fear, uncertainty, and difficulty. It provides the necessary elements we need, not just to survive but to thrive. We must be willing to face our fears together if we're to move forward together.

CHAPTER 8

Relate

People are Worth the R.I.S.K.

WHAT DOES IT LOOK like to interact with others in a way that validates dignity? The do's and don'ts are in chapter four and provide a high-level look at what it means to be with others and to put dignity front and center. But in practical terms and in everyday actions, what can we do to interact with our coworkers and teams in a way that makes us dignity champions?

As with any worthwhile and meaningful endeavor, we must determine that we will move in a given direction and be intentional about our behavior. When it comes to physical fitness, we can't simply wish we were fit or strong or have great endurance. We must lift or run or move our bodies in such a way that produces the thing we are after.

The same is true with our minds. Thinking dignity is a good idea or agreeing that dignity "works" isn't enough. We must put it into practice over and over again.

Because dignity is more than just a good idea, the cost is high and the challenge is difficult. Putting dignity into practice requires us to change and become vulnerable in ways we may not be accustomed to. Dignity involves risk. We risk being hurt. We risk being misunderstood. We risk having our own dignity violated. But we also have an opportunity. We may be able to validate someone's dignity in such a way that it ignites them and sets them on a completely positive trajectory. We could be the catalyst for change that makes all the difference in their life. It could be that their relationships turn around, their work improves, or simply that they look at the world in a more positive way.

Risks happen with any interaction, regardless of our intention and desires. They happen because we are human. So why not be intentional with how we interact with one another? Why not take the opportunity to validate dignity?

I am proposing that you take the R.I.S.K. Take the risk to put dignity first. Take the risk to close the dignity gap. Make dignity the central piece of how you think and act toward those you work with, live with, and love. They are worth the risk. And so are you.

Taking the risk with others means being intentional about our behavior. We have to learn how to **R**elate, gain **I**nsight, **S**erve and act with **K**indness as we put dignity first. Over the next few chapters, we will explore what they are and what they look like.

Our Need for Connection

Humans group together. We may have originally done this for protection, keeping safe from the environment and marauding tribes. But the truth is, regardless of the reason, we gravitate toward one another. We are social creatures. While individuals can survive on their own for a time, as a species humans require social interaction. When people live on their own, they can be quite happy and even productive. Monks of all types are an example of this. For whatever reason, they've decided to live apart from others and can do so quite successfully. Hermits are the same.

However, this is not the norm. The vast majority of people are together and connected with others in meaningful ways. Even those who want to withdraw from society will live in cloisters and small communities together. Ninety-nine percent of us need to be connected with others, even if it's as basic as the initial relationship of a mother and child.

There is a reason prisons use solitary confinement for punishment. Former Arizona senator and prisoner of war John McCain said, "It's an awful thing, solitary. It crushes your spirit and weakens your resistance more effectively than any other form of mistreatment."

Being together is critical for health and wellness. Anyone who has gone without human contact for a serious length of time desires a relationship, whether that is a simple conversation or physical contact.

Some people reading this may be thinking about how much they enjoy their alone time. They find being around people taxing, and they prefer their own routines and space. But there can come a time when being alone will equal being lonely. It's not a flaw; it's science. And loneliness can be deadly. Psychologist John Cacioppo, in his book *Loneliness: Human Nature and the Need for Social Connection*, points out that loneliness affects us emotionally and physically but the problem is deeper than that. He goes as far as saying it is as bad as obesity and smoking!

Through the ages, to stave off threats from their environments, people sought safety in numbers, which requires cooperation and the ability to live somewhat peaceably with one another. Even today, those who live in the remotest parts of the world count on neighbors to bail them out, or at the very least, to get or trade supplies.

A favorite bumper sticker says "coexist" spelled out with various religious symbols. Humans do coexist. We live together at the same time and in the same space. So, it isn't a matter that we do coexist; rather, it's a matter of *how* we coexist.

And the *how* matters as much as the *what*.

We are together in various states: together at work, at home, at play, or at war. There are any number of places and ways we are together coexisting. However, can we agree that we are at our best when we are *together*, especially together validating the dignity of those around us.

Humans are beautiful and fantastic creatures, capable of incredible acts of beauty and we have limitless potential. We learned how to put a man on the moon!

Unfortunately, we are also capable of unspeakable evil and hideous atrocities like war crimes and genocide.

Dignity points us towards our potential and our beauty. It unleashes us to be who we are in an unapologetic and creative way. Dignity frees us from constraints and allows us to dream and become. When we validate the dignity of family members, friends, and strangers, beautiful things happen. We can connect with anyone from anywhere on the planet when we choose dignity first. Our common humanity is the best starting place.

Again, dignity is important because it is the core of what it means to be human. We've gone through what it is, how to validate it, and how diversity and inclusion won't get us there on their own.

I am a big proponent of not just describing what's at stake, but also in helping people with the how. Anyone can talk about what to do but getting it into practice is where the rubber will meet the road.

Any endeavor worth its salt takes a risk, and there is much to be gained when pursuing the validation of dignity. People flourish, businesses become healthy, and relationships strengthen. Humanity wins on every level. But it takes risk and vulnerability on our part. We must lean into our fears and vulnerabilities to access another's dignity. As scary as that may feel, people are worth the risk. You are, too.

What follows is a step-by-step process to practice when working toward exercising the power of dignity.

R Stands for Relate

Step one is to seek to *relate* to the other person. You may not have anything in common, or you may not even like the person, so learning how to relate is the critical first step. Relate means to connect or to identify with. It means we gain the ability to see how we aren't so different from someone else.

Years ago, I spent a summer with several college students from around the States and Europe. We were quite the collection.

I distinctly remember the day when John arrived. His Ford Mustang 5.0 roared as it slid into the parking space. He was wearing pressed khakis, loafers, a matching belt, and a sharp polo shirt. His jet-black hair was perfectly in place and parted to the side. His Wayfarer sunglasses covered part of his handsome face as he took in his new environment.

I drew a quick comparison with myself and thought of my rapidly eroding Ford Tempo, my t-shirt and blue jeans. I immediately said to myself, "There's one guy I know I won't be friends with."

He was from UCLA. His dad was a lawyer. He *was* SoCal.

I was from the University of Montana and attended "Red Tractor High," as he liked to refer to it. My dad sold insurance, and I was from a place not many people had heard of. One person even said, "Montana. That's a state, right?"

How could a guy like me possibly relate to a guy like John?

As it turned out John and I became good friends. He and I spent the following summer in central Asia with another team of college students, and now we've been friends for nearly thirty years. He is wise, caring, intelligent, and hilarious. He loves people and cares deeply about how they look at the world.

I was able to relate to John, and he was able to relate to me. We connected around our common faith, care for people, and sense of humor. What I saw as significant obstacles were only differences, and as it turns out, they were minor at best. He's a good man and a good friend.

What we perceive as differences can cause massive problems with relating. Remember the Ladder of Inference and the steps our minds take toward increasing abstract thoughts which then lead us toward misguided beliefs? Here's how I moved up the ladder with John:

- I started with the observable data: John's appearance.
- I selected some details about his behavior: the car pulling in and John's confident demeanor.
- I added some meaning of my own: John is disinterested in connecting with someone like me.
- I made assumptions about him: John's cocky and arrogant.
- I concluded that John thinks people like me are beneath him.
- I now believed that John is someone I don't want to connect with.
- I reached the top of the ladder and did what I could to avoid him.

I am embarrassed to write the truth about my first encounter with John. I allowed my insecurities to drive me up the ladder very quickly. What only took seconds could have kept me from a lasting friendship. Had I kept John in the initial position I placed him, I would have relegated him to the sidelines. Worse, I could have made him an enemy. I wonder how many incredible friendships are missed because of this.

This happens more than we realize with disastrous consequences to various areas of our lives. Whatever environment we find ourselves in, with friends or family or coworkers, the Ladder of Inference is with us. It's how our brains work and how we think.

Here's an example using driving. You start your morning like any other morning. For the sake of argument, you are on time with no major hiccups, and nothing upsets you as you leave the house. Once you are on the road, you get in the appropriate traffic lane and ease into the morning commute. Suddenly a car appears out of nowhere and merges right in front of you. Once in your lane, it speeds down the road, weaving in and out of traffic. (By the way, this scenario plays out every single day where I live. If you don't live where people drive like their hair is on fire, try to imagine being cut off in traffic wherever you live.)

Let's look at the Ladder of Inference in this situation:
- Observable data: A car rapidly pulled in front of your car.
- Selected details about behavior: The car pulls out quickly, changing lanes and accelerating.
- Added meaning: The driver cares little for other drivers and me.
- Made assumptions: The driver is careless and dangerous.
- Draw conclusions: The driver thinks they are more important than anyone else.
- Form beliefs: The driver is a jerk, and I would like to give them a piece of my mind.
- Top of the ladder: I speed up to share my feelings with them.

This conclusion is reached within seconds, and because you haven't dissected the data or moved slowly up or down the ladder, you now have road rage and possible violence. Imagine your morning was not pristine: Spilled coffee, running late, kid's homework unfinished, a fight with a spouse, a sick dog, an unsettling phone call, a last-minute email, or any mixture of the above becomes a recipe for road disaster.

The truth is, this is where we reside. We are somewhere in this matrix all day, every day. We never know what is happening or what other people are experiencing. A quote attributed to author and minister John Watson says, "Be kind, for everyone you meet is fighting a hard battle." This can be difficult when we are fighting our own hard battles.

Now let's reframe the driving incident from the other perspective. It will change how we think and feel about it. It will help us *relate*.

You are attempting to leave the house on a regular morning, and if nothing goes wrong, you should arrive at work at your usual time.

But this morning, you slept in a bit because you helped your child with homework later than usual and took an emergency call from a family member that lasted much longer into the night than you expected.

You forgot to program the coffee the night before, and you don't have time to make it, so you decide to run through the local drive-thru for a cup of caffeine. That sets you back a few more minutes. You realize now the car is low on gas, and you have no choice but to stop; otherwise you won't make it work. So you stop to fill up, in line with all the other people in the same situation this morning.

Now on your way, much later than usual, the office calls with the news that the VP is making a surprise visit, and you are expected to be there with the team to greet them. While merging into traffic, driving faster than usual, you notice an object in the road that will damage your vehicle. So, you swerve into the other lane, just a bit ahead of the car behind you, avoiding the item you now recognize as a piece of tire from a semi-truck. Glancing in the rearview mirror, you see the person you "cut off" throw their hands up in disgust and despair. Since you *needed* to be in that lane to get to work and the angry driver is getting smaller in your mirror, you focus your attention on the road ahead and what you will say to the team and VP.

Can you *relate* to that? Have you ever had a morning like that? Have you ever done anything like that? I know I have, more than once.

Judge, Jury, and Executioner

We judge other people by their actions while we judge ourselves by our motivations.

Let me say that again.

We judge other people by their actions while we judge ourselves by our motivations.

It's a difficult truth to swallow.

We justify our behavior based on our internal drives, which we believe are inherently righteous. Everyone else is forced to judge our actions based on what they see. This dynamic makes the Ladder of Inference all the more tricky. It is nearly impossible to consider someone's motivation through their actions. It takes coming down the ladder, approaching that person, and asking questions about what is happening.

When we choose not to do this, we make enemies of the people around us, or if they don't become enemies, they are, at best, objects we move, ignore, or discard. They become problems and irritations we'd be better off without. From there, it doesn't take much for them to become the "other." The other is someone who is unlike us. They don't think like us or act like us, they don't like the same things we like or support what we support. They are subhuman.

And it's easy to do this in our increasingly polarized world as we lazily lump people into categories and groups while saying things like "they all do that." As if an entire group of people, comprised of a myriad of backgrounds, cultural differences, experiences, desires, and hurts, acts the same way. It's impossible.

When we head down this road, we enter dangerous territory because making people mere objects in our minds is a few steps from outright genocide. It is this simple...

Our Thoughts -> (those people are stupid)

Our Actions -> (I actively avoid, hinder, and talk about them in this way)

Our Practice -> (I am in the habit of behaving the same way each time the person or topic comes up)

Subhuman -> treat in any manner we choose (the 'other person' becomes unworthy of any type of human treatment)

The Armenian genocide, the Jewish Holocaust, and the Rwandan genocide are just a few examples, among far too many, of this dynamic. This behavior is the worst of humanity, and it's scary how quickly things can turn horrid.

Let's pull us back from this brink of disaster a bit and examine the small ways this impacts us.

Think about the divisions in the workplace. Depending on your context, there are frontline workers, managers, bosses, directors, VPs, or C-suite executives. Ever heard someone say, "Those execs only care about themselves and making money. They don't care about people like us?" Or how about the accountants? "They don't care about anything but the numbers and the budget." Maybe at home, it's teenagers. "They never consider others." If not at work or home, how about the generalities we make about the different sexes? These gross generalities are easy to fall into…to our detriment.

Choosing to *relate* to your boss, coworker, or family member means taking a step toward embracing dignity. Imagine your relationships with a different level of connectedness at work, when you relate and see things from their perspective. You won't have to paint your manager or fellow employees in a bad light or call them names. Instead, you start to *relate* to them. You see them differently because at the end of the day you are not that different.

We share about 99.9 percent of DNA with those around us. We all need food, water, and shelter. Oxygen is a given. Everyone has hopes and dreams, things we love and dislike. Our similarities are so prevalent that it makes you wonder why we tend to focus on the differences so much. In fact, we don't just focus on our differences; we point them out as a way to make sure there is a decent division between us, keeping us safe from one another. I am all for seeing the differences, but they should be celebrated, not used as an excuse for terrible behavior.

Our differences make us beautiful and worthy of wonder. Choosing to *relate* and press into our similarities keeps us at the bottom of the Ladder of Inference and allows grace for one another. We can talk about people's behavior, which can change, rather than talking about their identity as if they are the flaw.

CHAPTER 9

Insight
People are Worth the R.I.S.K.

A FRIEND OF MINE WAS often in charge of putting on regional events. Adults and students would gather from a tri-state area for a few days of training, practice, and projects to implement what they learned. This was followed by a week-long service project somewhere in or near the U.S.

The logistics were crazy, and the detail list long. His preference was to operate in the tasks, not necessarily the people. He didn't mind being upfront, helping people orient to the day or what was happening next, but he struggled in the transition moving from large group to small group.

He and I had both taken DISC assessments (DISC is an acronym for Dominance, Influence, Steadiness, and

Compliance). The evaluation is based on the work of Carl Jung.
- Dominance measures how you respond to problems and challenges.
- Influence measures how you influence people and contacts to your point of view.
- Steadiness tells you how you react to change in terms of pace and consistency.
- Compliance tells you how you respond to rules and procedures set by others.

Everyone has a high and low end in each category and a preference of which they use. My friend's preference was the D category, which means he likes a fast pace, immediate problem solving, and getting things done. Occasionally plans required a pivot as the logistics of that many people performing that many tasks are not set in stone. When those pivots happened, my friend focused more on the problem and less on the people. He missed key communication points, overlooked how people felt, and left others in his wake while trying to complete the necessary tasks. It wasn't uncommon for people to get upset or confront him due to this behavior.

Because we were friends and had a common language using DISC, we developed a code.

There is a children's story called *Heidi* about a little girl who lived in the Swiss Alps. His assessment showed that his Dominance trait was very high. In other words, he had a high D, so when he began leaving others in his wake, I pulled him aside and told him his little Swiss girl was running amok (a "high D" equals Heidi).

Ever work with anyone like that who goes charging up the mountain to solve a problem but causes all sorts of issues as they do it? It is critical to have others around them to rein them in occasionally.

His response was often, "Really?" To which I affirmed what was happening. Luckily, he was aware enough to adjust his behavior and began asking for help, apologizing where needed, and communicating more effectively.

I – Insight

This is why *insight* is so essential. Learning about yourself and how others see you allows you to be present to them and the situation and to champion the dignity of those around you.

Maybe you've seen the opposite. You've been in situations where a leader or someone you know has certain off-putting behaviors. Some see it, while others are oblivious. Some, like my friend, simply need a reminder.

Without *insight*, people get hurt, run into "brick walls," keep making the same mistakes, and cause employee turnover. It doesn't have to be this way. Dignity gives us courage to look at others and ourselves in a new light. If *relate* is looking outward toward those around us, *insight* is the ability to look at ourselves and our behaviors.

There is a saying in business: "People don't quit jobs. They quit managers." When leaders in critical positions lack insight, they push good people away.

Here is an example: Amy works in the corporate space and is frustrated with her job. She is intelligent, educated, articulate, and has a great deal to offer the company. New ideas for improvement and cost-saving measures come to her mind, and when implemented, produce what she expected. Unfortunately, Amy's new manager Kathy is not a detailed person. Kathy likes people and is happy to have them in her office or sit down over lunch. She is more of a big-picture thinker who is very persuasive. Amy has reminded Kathy of crucial details for an upcoming project more than once and has noticed that they have not yet come through. Amy has even shown Kathy how to track the details if necessary, but Kathy keeps missing them. Kathy's lack of punctuality to meetings and seemingly glib responses leaves Amy feeling frustrated that her new boss appears incapable. Even more frustrating is that everyone appears to like Kathy; her easygoing manner and willingness to chit-chat make her approachable and friendly.

Eventually though, Kathy's behavior begins to impact more than Amy. Others notice her lack of attention to detail and wind up covering for her at important meetings or work late to finish what she missed. In addition, they are less patient than Amy and more willing to be vocal with their problems. Amy and others are thinking about finding new work. Despite their best efforts at communicating their frustrations to Kathy and her superiors, nothing is changing. Their departure will leave significant roles in the organization unfilled. The cost will be high. With each employee departure, the company loses trust and knowledge and income-generating potential.

Or how about a boss, colleague, or friend who has one way of doing things? They might as well have a placard on their desk that reads "my way or the highway." They squelched ideas and dismissed time and money-saving ventures, leaving the employees feeling helpless. There was little joy, hope, or community as everyone laid low to keep from getting blasted and just worked to survive. I've been in organizations like this where everyone has to orient around the boss and their day completely depended on the boss's mood.

Intent Vs. Impact

How much would it change if the leaders gained some *insight*? It can start with intent versus impact, which relates to judging others by their actions and judging ourselves by our motivations. It looks like this:

Our intent: Get the job finished.
Our impact: People feel run over and hurt.

or

Our intent: Show compassion.
Our impact: Comes across as ingenuine.

or

Our intent: Help someone with a problem.
Our impact: They believe we think they are stupid.

Most, if not all of us, have good intentions. Our desire isn't to hurt, embarrass, or belittle anyone. We typically aren't out to harm. However, we can easily have that effect and create a problem. Without *insight*, we stay in a cycle of behavior that doesn't deliver what we hope. It does the opposite.

I can bring the *insight* discussion a little closer to home. It's not uncommon for my kids or my wife to come home and talk about their day. I get to grasp better what they experienced and how they are doing when we chat while cooking or even catch up on a quick phone call during a commute.

I try to ask open-ended and feeling questions that draw out a bit more detail, so as to avoid responses like "fine" or "good." One-word answers don't tell us much. Inevitably my family will talk about the problems they encountered with either a task or a person. They describe their feelings of hurt or frustration as I listen closely. I love my wife and kids, and I want the best for them, so I want to help when I hear that things went poorly or unfairly. In such situations I ask how they responded, hoping they were able to fix the problem and prevent the pain. I ask them how the person or situation changed according to their efforts. I ask them if they tried solutions A, B, or C, knowing that they would be better off if they did what I suggest.

After some time, I noticed a change in my wife. Her frustration began to target me. I couldn't understand what the problem was until finally, she said, "Sometimes I just need you to listen." Those words echo in my head every time now when I sit with a friend or a client. I intended to help her, but my impact made her, and sometimes my kids, feel like I wasn't listening. I was communicating that I didn't care about how they felt. It was crushing, but I knew it was true. I lacked *insight*. Instead of validating their emotions and being present, I tried to ease my pain at their frustration by fixing it.

Over time, I learned to ask a critical question, which, it turns out, helps with *insight* and embraces the power of dignity. I now ask, "Would you like me to listen? Or would you like me to solve?" If they say, "listen," I press in with active listening, ask clarifying and open-ended questions, and I don't offer solutions. It's been a hard lesson to learn and an even more complex skill to develop, but it's been worth it.

It's easy to lack *insight* when you assume you know what the other person needs.

Everyone can benefit from more *insight*. Learning about ourselves and applying the data in meaningful ways is a game-changer. When working with teams, leaders, or other groups, the "aha" moments are the best. Watching the light bulb go on when working through a behavioral assessment or an emotional intelligence brief is incredibly rewarding. Helping them implement change is even better. I've experienced the benefit of gaining insight in my own life, and I've watched it do the same for countless others.

Certain personalities may have a bit more difficulty in thinking "dignity first" than others. Having insight into our personalities and how we are wired is enormously important. This helps us know our tendencies and preferences. It doesn't lock us into cages; it frees us.

People with a preference for tasks first may look past the person in any given situation. Their eye is on what needs to be done, not necessarily who is doing it. People with a high D or C in the DISC profile may tend toward things and problem-solving. This is a great strength and much needed in our workspaces and relationships. However, this tendency requires a pause to consider the people behind the task: How are they thinking and feeling, and what does this situation look like from their perspective?

Those with high I and S in DISC may think people first and have an easier time bringing dignity into the conversation. So, how is this freeing?

Knowing how you are wired and what your preferences are as you enter a situation gives you the ability to choose how you behave. You aren't shackled to unknown behaviors and motivations. You are free to choose how you respond to those around you in any given situation. This agency leads to better decision-making and better relationships.

Here for Impact

Have you wondered why you are here? You're in good company if you have. A Google search yields about 4,260,000,000 results for this question in 0.6 seconds. This isn't some existential blackhole, but a fundamental question because there is not always a clear purpose for why we are standing in a certain room or seated in a certain chair. There's a reason we're in a corner office or a closet with a broom. The reason might be implied by our title or stated by the people who placed us there, but searching out the role we play in any given situation is normal and extremely important.

Regardless of the titles and positions, we are all here for influence and impact, and that influence and impact happens through our relationships with one another. Influence and impact take place through our ideas and actions, through our words or what we create.

No matter how it's transferred, you are here for the influence and impact only you can bring.

As a manager at work, you may lead people in a change process, followed by providing a listening ear to a peer struggling with a direct report, and then find yourself following through on another project for your boss. Each has a different skill set, but the same opportunity for influence.

When you sit with friends, you might also have an impact in the ways you listen, give advice, and empathize.

With your family, you may provide leadership for your kids, give direction for the crucial "household" decisions that chart the foreseeable future, and comfort your significant other after a tough day.

These are all ways you have influence and impact.

Being human means being in relationships, and relationships mean influence and impact. How much and in what direction is where the rubber meets the road.

We all have influence, and if leadership equals influence, then it isn't a question of *if* we are a leader. The question becomes, how do we lead? How we influence and impact those around us shapes our leadership. (This doesn't speak to the amount of influence and impact we may have; simply that all of us have it.)

The maxim is correct: The *how* is as important as the *what*. How we influence and impact those around us matters. Either we complete a task but with a trail of bodies in our wake, or we achieve a mission while growing and encouraging others along the way. The how matters.

When it comes to dignity, *how* is everything. It's virtually impossible to celebrate someone's dignity while running them over at the same time. Taking others into account when completing a task, implementing a project, or negotiating a workload means being in their shoes. Validating their emotions and listening to their concerns go a long way in building trust and serving people. Good leaders learn to do this and put it into practice daily. It's projects *and* people, not one or the other.

Do me a favor. Take a minute to consider a couple of things. Look at your fingerprint. It's unique to you. While some may have many similarities, no one has your print attached to your finger, hand, arm, body, or mind. You make a unique contribution to those around you because no one is exactly like you. You may do things similarly to others, but no one will do it the *way* you do it.

Now think about your laugh. Have you ever identified someone by their laugh? Some are loud, some snort, and some wheeze. We all have different laughs. Laughs are a core part of who we are. When was the last time you belly laughed? I bet others laughed with you—because it's contagious. This is what gaining insight does. It helps us connect with others by learning about them, laughing with them, and seeing them in a fresh way. Insight helps us to see below the surface and recognize there is more to us and more to those around us.

We make a unique impact on our world simply by being who we are. Imagine what we can do when we decide to look at others that way? Imagine what happens in them and us when we unleash the power of dignity.

CHAPTER 10

Serving
People are Worth the R.I.S.K.

THE POWER OF DIGNITY in practice looks like service. All of us are in service. We may not think we orient our lives this way, but it is reality.

Think about it like this. Every day that we participate in work, we are serving the purposes of the company in some way. We are in service to the mission, vision, and values of our workplaces. We are in service to our customers and fellow employees. Our jobs aren't just about us, but also about those we work with and to whom we deliver goods and services. We are in service to shareholders and stakeholders. More people are invested in our success than we know, and they are as keen to flourish as we are. We are in service to our teams, managers, and peers.

We are here to lead through our unique influence and impact, and servant-leadership is the way forward when choosing to honor dignity.

Servant-Leadership

Perhaps you recoil at the idea of servanthood. It sounds like a denigrating position with little impact to you. Servants are here for your bidding, not the other way around; they are to execute your ideas and implement your plans.

While some might choose to manage this way, they will likely see a high turnover rate and loads of inefficiency and disengagement because a top-down approach only "works" for those on top. If this is you, I encourage you to flip the script. The servant-leader frees those accountable to them to make decisions and create change. They give away responsibility and the power to implement.

Invariably, servant-leaders are enormously popular and garner a high degree of trust. This is because they don't just concern themselves with what gets done, but how it happens. I know a C-suite executive of a large international organization with enormous impact and influence. He sees himself at the service of everyone in the organization. He sees how the success of the cleaning team relates to the fulfillment of the company's mission.

Another *Fortune 500* CEO imparts dignity another way. He takes the time to ask the janitor and the barista handing him his morning coffee what their names are (and remembers them!), about their families, and how their days are going. He does this with just as much interest as he does his executive leadership team.

Jon Picoult in an article for Forbes.com cites a University of Iowa study that found "while a business' financial success did help improve employee engagement, the relationship *was stronger* in the other direction. Employee engagement drove financial success more materially than the reverse relationship. In short, these researchers found that happy and engaged employees are indeed a precursor to business success, not a by-product of it."[23]

When dignity is validated, people flourish. When people flourish, businesses (comprised of people) flourish. Study upon study shows this relationship between employee satisfaction and the bottom line.

Servant-leadership validates dignity in everyone within our sphere of influence and increases employee satisfaction, engagement, and retention.

Balancing people and projects isn't easy. We work with people, but our projects measure us. Many metrics measure time, efficiency, profit, or other quantifiable data points. Those tools don't measure trust, engagement, growth in courage, expanded capacities, or empathy. Another set of tools is required, and companies are working hard in this direction with engagement and satisfaction surveys because they know those aspects of work affect the bottom line.

Further, Millennials are the largest group in the workforce today, and they are not simply satisfied with getting a paycheck. They value whole-person engagement, development, company culture, and making a difference in the world. Being productive isn't enough.

---

23 – Jon Picoult, "Are Engaged Employees A Driver Of Business Success Or A Consequence Of It?," Forbes, November 11, 2019, https://www.forbes.com/sites/jonpicoult/2019/11/11/are-engaged-employees-a-driver-of-business-success-or-a-consequence-of-it.

The next generations will expect no less. Businesses must adjust. Emphasis on whole-person health, physical, mental, and spiritual aspects are becoming the norm. Understanding the needs of employees outside work fosters empathy and gives the employer/employee relationship more pliability. Servant-leaders give grace, knowing people are wearing several hats. Today, many work remotely, become homeschool families, tend to loud pets during Zoom meetings, and engage in essential tasks while their partner is on a video chat.

A top-down, business-needs-only approach in today's workplace climate doesn't meet the whole person's needs and indeed doesn't champion dignity.

When you see people in their dignity, people are not resources to be used—they are potential to be realized. Extraterrestrial sci-fi films tell the story of an alien culture encountering our species and planet to either suck the resources dry or use the people in some nefarious plot. Have we heard of companies doing the same thing? Maybe you've been a part of one; perhaps you are part of one right now.

Influencing from among, not above, means we know the people we work with. Understanding their key strengths and weaknesses can help you put them in the best places for them to succeed. Asking them what their goals are for their positions and careers enables you to equip them for the journey they are taking with you. Encouraging them to pursue their passions inside and outside the workplace helps them see that you're for them and that you're there to serve them. We don't always have to develop the plan, but we can put some wind in their sails to help them get there by asking: How can I help you win? What can I do to help you in this next season? What next step can I help you take? These are the types of questions servant-leaders get to ask and get to help answer.

Servant-leaders celebrate others. Celebrating when those in your influence reach a goal or overcome a challenge takes servant-leaders to the next level. It's one thing to help someone get somewhere; it's another thing to pause and celebrate their wins.

Celebration looks like speaking their language. Buy them a small gift. Write them a note by hand (and an email kudo). Praise them in front of their peers and people of great influence. Take them to lunch or give them a simple handshake. When celebrating them, be specific. Don't just say "good job" or "way to go." Tell them what they did. "You handled that project perfectly by_____." "Your key insight _____ made a major difference to _____." Help them and others have a clear picture of why you are celebrating them. Having insight into how your people tick and what they value allows you to celebrate with them in a way that makes sense to them.

It's more than the thought that counts. It's cute when the five-year-old boy "buys" his mom a Tonka Truck for her birthday. We easily forgive children for mistaking what they like for what we want. But as leaders, it makes us look silly. Just because it speaks your language doesn't mean it speaks theirs. Learn about the people in your sphere of influence.

One of the best job titles I've seen is that of CEO: Chief Encouragement Officer. The title implies the person who brings courage to those around them. It communicates connection with employees and positions the title-bearer as someone who will cheer for others. Positioning ourselves relationally instead of structurally helps build trust and gives us a chance to maximize the gifts of the people we work with. This creates a win-win dynamic. People exercising their talents at work get celebrated for doing so. This environment creates better workplace satisfaction and better results.

It isn't that job titles will define what we do or how we do it. For example, there are plenty of chief executive officers who function like chief encouragement officers. However, labels can change the culture in a workplace environment and speak to how intentional we may choose to behave.

Actions and attitudes shape environments as much as anything. *How* we do what we do is as important as *what* we do. Servant-leadership sets the stage and the standard for how people function and interact with one another. Nothing greases the gears better than people serving one another in an effort to accomplish tasks. Inversely, when everyone is out for themselves, things don't run smoothly.

Take a moment and consider how you are leading those around you. How are people experiencing your impact? Unleashing the power of dignity means we remember the quote "attitude reflects leadership."[24] Serving those around you will create a culture of service.

---

24 – *Remember the Titans*. Directed by Boaz Yakin, performance by Denzel Washington, Walt Disney Pictures, 2000.

CHAPTER 11

Kindness

People are Worth the R.I.S.K.

MEDIEVAL JAPAN MAY NOT be the first place people think of when they think about kindness. Across Europe and Asia, the medieval period was full of trial, difficulty, disease, and violence. Hardly the recipe for something like beauty and culture and kindness.

Yet, humans tend to produce beauty from ashes in many ways. Cultural explosions often follow difficult times as if the human spirit breaks through in a need to express itself.

The Ashikaga Period, also known as the Muromachi Period, lasted from 1338–1573 under the Ashikaga Shogunate. During this time, even while not experiencing perfect peace, some important Japanese cultural expressions were born.

Kindness and Kintsugi

One of the most significant expressions was the development of the tea ceremony. This highly involved process of making and experiencing Japan's green tea remains today despite its various iterations and the number of years that have passed since its origin. Over the course of time, influences from China and Zen Buddhism were married to Japanese customs and cultures.

In a unique blend of these ingredients, Shogun Yashimasa created something beautiful. Every part of the tea ceremony is essential and imbued with dignity: It isn't just what you do; it's how you do it. Attention to detail goes into every aspect; a far cry from grabbing a chai-tea at the local coffee shop.

Yashimasa was particularly fond of the *tenmoku* cups, which master ceramists made. These cups were round and low, providing a pleasing aesthetic. The cup was as important, if not more important, than the tea itself. When the tea master filled the cup, he rotated it carefully, and the tea slowly and intentionally poured into the cup. When full, the fortunate recipient would praise the beauty of the cup. Think of your favorite coffee mug, but on steroids. These cups were important.

In what seems to be a twist of fate, and what was certainly an uncomfortable moment, Yahshimasa's favorite cup fell from his hands and broke into pieces.

Ceramics was still a rare skill in Japan but widely practiced in China, where the most skillful masters lived. Yashimasa's servants handed the broken pieces over to the Chinese for repair. The standard practice was to "sew" the pieces back together by making holes on each side of the crack and running thin iron thread through the holes to hold the ceramic pieces together. While this "fixed" the broken pieces and restored the cup, it was not pleasing to the eye or even to the hand.

When Yahshimasa saw the "repaired" cup, he was livid. The cup was ugly and void of the character he wanted in his ceremony. Despite their lack of expertise, the Japanese ceramists took up the challenge and did all they could to repair the cup. They used the sap from a local tree as an adhesive, creating a type of lacquer. The lacquer filled in the cracks, and in a move of incredible brilliance, they covered the lacquered cracks with gold dust. The result was a tenmoku cup with veins of gold running in and through the cup.

When the inexperienced ceramists presented their cup to Yahshimasa, he was overjoyed at the repair. Not only was this beautiful, but it had a new life. The repair recognized the imperfections in the cup and revealed a new way of being beautiful, and made the cup completely unique.

Thus, the art of *kintsugi* was born: repairing broken ceramics with gold. Not only was the cup usable, but it was also a piece of art.

Why all this talk about medieval Japanese cups? Because *kintsugi* and kindness go together. All of us have a purpose. All of us possess dignity. Yet, we're all cracked, fractured, broken, and in some cases shattered. Our dignity is violated by significant, life-altering events or through increments of time creating small fissures within us. We are fragile despite our remarkable resilience and value.

Our standard means of dealing with broken things is to sweep them up and throw them in the trash. But sometimes we can do what the Chinese ceramic masters did—a crude yet effective means of restoring who we are and how we function: Those extra holes and iron thread work on the surface but don't restore and renew beauty the way *kintsugi* can.

Kindness works like *kintsugi*. It recognizes a person's inherent value, like the Shogun's favorite tenmoku cup, and treats them as such. Ask yourself: Do you treat the people around you like they are precious and valuable, or are they just a means to an end?

In business, people often believe they don't have the time or energy for this kind of kindness: We are a business, not a counseling center (unless, of course, your business is a counseling center), so who has time to put people back together with such care and concern? My job and my boss don't care about the gold veins in the people; they care about the bottom line—no money, no people.

While this sentiment is partially true, no one assumes you are a master at *kintsugi*. Yet. Everyone has a role to play in kindness and putting people back together with gold. Your part may be to kindly recognize the cracks and treat those around you with gentility. Maybe you see the brokenness as it is laid out in the open, ready for the refuse bin. Perhaps you are the one who can hold the brokenness of those around you while someone else applies the lacquer.

This is not about company policy and laws protecting employees. Those are crucial. This is about a kindness that goes beyond policy and law. A kindness that looks like a phone call, text message, email, flowers, or best wishes that let people know they matter even when they are unable to perform their job the way they normally do. It's the way you welcome them back after an absence or the grace you give them when they ask for time off.

Kindness breeds loyalty and trust, and that's not something you can buy. It has to come from who you are and from the culture you build.

Kindness recognizes flaws but doesn't emphasize them, for flaws reside in each of us and like the cup with golden veins, we are all unique and beautiful. If all we do is orient negatively to one another's brokenness, we will never participate in the power of dignity, and our indifference to the whole person will create a dynamic where people feel unheard and uncared for. Employees who believe that the company and the people they work with don't care don't last long, and this failure perpetuates the cycle of hiring, on-boarding, training, difficulty, departure, and hiring. The turnover is a killer to business and culture.

Kindness is risky, but it's worth it.

Seeing Isn't Believing

It's wise to remember that brokenness will not always reveal itself the way we think. It's easy to see a broken cup on the floor or a crack in our cup when tea leaks on the table. But sometimes brokenness is less subtle but requires no less kindness.

Not long ago, I was running on a treadmill. During this particular session, I decided to push a little faster and challenge myself a bit more. I increased the speed and adjusted the uphill angle. As I ran, the sweat was flying, and my heart was pumping. I felt pretty good about myself, thinking about how many calories I must be burning and how fast

I was getting. These thoughts all came to a screeching halt when I heard and felt a pop in my left knee.

Suddenly, my awareness focused on the burning pain in my knee as I slowed the treadmill down. My run turned to a walk and my walk to a limp. I finished my workout but with a realization that something serious happened.

Over the next several weeks, I nursed my knee along with ice and ibuprofen, hoping it would improve. However, when the popping, locking, and grinding continued, I knew I needed to see a doctor. We tried some physical therapy and some cortisone, but they had limited effects in remedying the symptoms.

What people observed was a slight limp, but they could not see what was happening on the inside. I looked okay, like I should be able to work out and run, but I wasn't functioning correctly.

The doctor ordered an MRI.

MRI, or magnetic resonance imaging, is a way for a physician to see what is happening with the soft tissue inside a joint or any other part of the body. With this information, doctors can have greater certainty about next steps for treatment.

When it comes to dignity and treating people with kindness, we need to use this approach. We need to give each other MRIs.

No, I am not advocating carrying bulky medical equipment around and insisting people get inside so we can see what's happening. I *am* advocating for a way of interpreting what we see.

On the outside, I had a limp. On the inside, my cartilage was torn in two places. This is how it is for most of us, yet we can adjust and adapt because we are strong and capable. Even so, it's possible to see when people have the ceramic of their lives put back together with medieval "sewing," and when it comes to kindness, it's best that we apply the M.R.I. (the most respectful interpretation) of what we observe.

It's easy to jump to conclusions about people and their behavior and attitudes. All of us do it (i.e., the Ladder of Inference). So, to act with kindness, we must ask ourselves, "What is the most respectful interpretation of what I am seeing?"

It's easy to dismiss broken things and throw away cracked vessels, but doing so means we are also at risk of meeting the garbage bin! We cannot know what is fully happening on the inside, but we can act with kindness when we see a crack or a limp.

The Three Strikes

Maybe there is someone at work or home or someplace in between who is a challenge for you to think respectfully about. You have given them one chance after another and exercised patience and kindness on repeat, but things just aren't working. Kindness doesn't mean the absence of conflict. Sometimes it means we care about one another enough to have difficult conversations.

I follow a few simple cues when I observe and experience complex or problematic behavior and need to apply the kindness principle.

The first time I chalk it up to being with other humans. No one is perfect, and these things happen. It may be a slight offense or large offense, but giving people the benefit of the doubt is the way forward. Depending on the day or how serious I see things, I may bring it to their attention and let them know how I feel about their behavior. Calling the manager the first time we are grieved may not be the best course of action, depending on the issue.

The second time it happens, I take note and chalk it up to coincidence, even if my gut tells me something different. I tend to listen to my gut. Ancient people thought it was the source of being human, and while I don't go that far, I listen carefully to what my gut says. Coincidences are part of life, and while some are unhappy coincidences, they happen, and I would rather apply the M.R.I. Taking this approach also keeps you from thinking of yourself as a victim and only looking for the other shoe to drop. At this point, I let them know I have a problem with their behavior.

If it happens a third time, I will ask to have a conversation. We are beyond being human or a simple coincidence. Now we need to figure out how to be together.

This process is kindness in action. More often than not, letting others know how you experience their behavior causes a connection, not a disconnect, and a willingness to work with one another. When people tell me about something I'm doing that is causing an issue, I'm ultimately happy to hear it. I prefer to know I'm the reason for someone's pain or discomfort so I can adjust my behavior. (This is the route to take interpersonally. When things reach the human resources or administrative level, you need conflict resolution and mediation. Both are critical skills and processes that, if done well, can drip with kindness.)

A word about kindness and weakness. You may think to yourself, "That is all well and good, but where I live and work, kindness gets chewed up and spit out." Many environments are not engineered to promote kindness; they are designed to produce things and results. You are not measured by how kind you are; rather, you are measured by how many sales you make, widgets you create, or deadlines you beat. Kindness is an afterthought.

In fact, you may think the idea of R.I.S.K. is too much. You've worked too hard and sacrificed too much to get to where you are to lose out because you are "nice." You have to be tough to make it where you are today. Choosing to *relate*, gain *insight*, *serve* and act with *kindness* looks like a weakness. It would be nothing but blood in the water for the sharks that circle around me.

I've heard this often. Unfortunately, the arguments against vulnerability, dignity, and choosing R.I.S.K. tend to fall into the same category: fear. Remember chapter seven on fear? What are you afraid of? Are you afraid of what might happen if you choose to champion the dignity of others? Or of what might happen if you choose to view yourself as possessing dignity? Once your fear is out in the open, it helps to talk about it and see what is really at risk. Hearing others' perspectives on your fears can show you that your fears are less dangerous than they appear.

We share a common worth, and the way we interact with one another can ensure that dignity wins. Once again, it isn't just what we do; it is how we do it. I am not advocating a naive and simple way of being—just the opposite, in fact. Choosing R.I.S.K. is an intentional and incredibly powerful way of living, working, and being. It bears a strength that doesn't require defensive positions and protective measures. It brings presence without walls up and ammunition ready. No jaws are clenched, or fists balled up.

CHAPTER 12

Dignity's Power in Story
Finding Dignity in Each Other's Stories

I LOVE LISTENING TO A good story. Sitting around with friends or acquaintances, sharing tales, and laughing is a great way to spend time. Through it we connect. We share an experience, not just of the moment but also in the space of the stories. We relate with one another, and I find that those around me aren't all that dissimilar from me.

Stories work like that. They are part of what it means to be human, and through stories we intersect with one another without much work or worry. They are powerful and important.

Connecting over every day experiences deepens relationships: Who hasn't been frustrated with a coworker? Who hasn't discovered an incredible place they love? Who hasn't heard a funny anecdote? Our experiences form a fabric of connection with those around us.

There is another story, though, sometimes revealed as we share stories. You might catch a glimpse of it on someone's face, in a downward glance, or in a gentle sigh. While stories are shared with others, another narrative is running through people's hearts and minds. This is the "other side" of the story, the story we tell ourselves.

The Story in Our Own Minds

It is not unlike the operating system on your computer. You interact with various applications as you go online, listen to music, or type a blog post; these are the things you see or hear, like the story being shared in a circle of friends. But behind the applications on your computer is the unseen operating system: Windows for those PC types, macOS for those who prefer Apple products, and Linux for…well, I have no idea who uses Linux. These systems affect every way in which you interact with your computer, like which apps work and what programs run. These systems help your computer operate efficiently and they update from time to time for optimal functioning.

The stories we tell ourselves work in a similar fashion—in the background, affecting the way we think, act, and feel. They inform us about the information we take in and change the way we interpret data.

For example, you get the news that cutbacks are happening at work. A simple statement—cutbacks are happening at work—can quickly turn it into a narrative in your head that reinforces what you already believe about yourself. The story may be filled with statements like: I'm not that valuable; they are going to find out I'm not that good at my job; my efforts don't matter; I don't deserve a job this good; I'll never amount to anything; or I suck. When cutbacks at work lead a storyline with these headers, things start to look different. Fear creeps in. The narratives around worthlessness grow stronger. A foreboding hangs over you, and you finally convince yourself that you're worth nothing, you're just an object. Next thing you know, you are searching LinkedIn for a new job in southern New Mexico as a hot chili tester at a drastic pay cut even though this news may not even affect you!

Imagine selling a computer whose operating system said upon start up, "I suck." Or in the hip, Mac-ish vernacular: iSuck. It would be a tough sell. No one would buy a computer with an operating system that said, "I suck." The reviews would be terrible. Yet, many of us run on this narrative. Data reaches our ears and finds a theme in our head, which then runs its course that deepens the dreaded story lines we tell ourselves.

But let's say the information about cutbacks reaches you, but the story lines say something like: I can adapt; I will survive (enter Gloria Gaynor); I am worthy of a great job; I am capable and smart; or I can handle this. Here, the news of cutbacks lands in fertile soil with opportunity for growth.

Everyone is somewhere in between these two ends of the spectrum. Both types of story lines operate behind the scenes, interpreting data and spitting out conclusions. Fear drives us one way; excitement and opportunity drive us another. Data is simply data.

Conclusions and Emotional Intelligence

Drawing conclusions on data and assigning it value that will reinforce narratives is what we do, and it's essential work. Maybe you're aware of how data comes to you; maybe you are not. Either way, that data is interpreted. Try to separate yourself from the most recent data you received. Was it about your health? A friend? Work-related? How did you interpret that data? Did it fall into a story that operates behind the scenes creating fear or excitement? Did you react at all? How did you feel afterward? What did you think?

The ability to pull the data apart from our conclusions is a critical life skill. When we don't work at this separation, we lack self-awareness and re-enforce a story we tell ourselves, which in turn perpetuates a low Emotional Intelligence. Constantly repeating this process leaves us in the dark and in the dust—not only do we lack awareness, but we fall behind others who have a better understanding of themselves, their emotions, and their social situations.

According to Daniel Goleman, Emotional Intelligence comprises five separate but interrelated skills.[25]

- Self-awareness: knowing one's strengths, weaknesses, drives, values, and impact on others
- Self-regulation: controlling or redirecting disruptive impulses and moods
- Motivation: relishing achievement for its own sake
- Empathy: understanding other people's emotional makeup
- Social skill: building rapport with others to move them in desired directions

---

[25] – Daniel Goleman, *What Makes a Leader?* (Harvard Business Review Press, 2017).

The good thing is, we can grow in each of these areas and can do the work of pulling apart the information from our conclusions and our emotions. We can assess how our "operating systems" are working; we can see when we are simply reacting or even overreacting. We are not slaves to our operating systems; they can get updates and upgrades. We can ask if we like what the systems are producing and what we might need to do to make them work the way we want. We get to choose how the data gets interpreted and how it may or may not reinforce the stories we tell ourselves.

This skill is essential because the stories we tell ourselves are the most powerful and influential stories of all. They are tied to our identity and our dignity, and they may be a validation or violation of both.

Because story is so powerful and such an integral part of being human, consider not just the stories you tell your friends and colleagues, but consider the stories you tell yourself. When was the last time you gave your system an update? When you get that update, you give yourself the opportunity to connect with yourself in a new way *and* open the possibility that the people around you aren't all that different from you. Knowing your story, how you think and "tick," makes it easier to be with others. You take an unknown out of the equation and give any interaction an opportunity to be more than a simple transaction (although those simple ones are important as well).

We are stories. Our experiences, relationships, and thoughts about ourselves make a tapestry of who we are. The stories we tell ourselves are important because they either validate or violate our dignity. We can see ourselves as a victim, friend, overcomer, truth-teller, or any number of things. The truth is, we're a little bit of everything. We aren't made up of just one thing; we are many different things. Which is why story is so important.

Our stories are not all that different. "Wait. You're a human? Me too! Wait. You need oxygen? Me too! Wait. You had important relationships? Me too! Wait. You want what's best for your loved ones? Me too!" If we can see our own stories and what they mean, we have the chance to champion our own dignity, and as we are able to do that, we can listen to others more easily. We can then give them the chance to tell their stories and learn about them, see the way they see themselves and ways we connect. In this way we champion their dignity as well as our own.

Entering Stories: Drugs

"Do you believe in God?" The question echoed from a stall in the men's room.

To say I was a bit alarmed is putting it mildly. I don't usually field these kinds of questions in these kinds of moments. Normally, I am in front of someone, or a group of someones, or online, talking about life and faith. Maybe I'm wearing a clerical collar (occupational hazard) or speaking at a church. This time, I was at a urinal in the bathroom, and it was the last thing I thought I would hear.

The question came from the stall farthest from me. A million different scenarios raced through my head, including some in which shootings were involved.

I slowly turned around to see who asked the question. I wasn't ready for what I saw.

Close to me, but not too close, was a young man, a bit emaciated and disheveled. He had an inordinate amount of clothing on, especially for Phoenix weather. He carried what looked like a cup of soup in one hand and held his pants up with the other.

"I do," I responded, uncertain of what I was facing.

He asked, "Can you pray for me? I need help."

"Of course," I said, "how can I pray?"

He told me the heartbreaking story of a young man with potential but caught up in drug addiction. He told me how he felt trapped and scared. In fact, when he heard me come into the bathroom, he quickly tried to flush his drug paraphernalia down the toilet (I remembered hearing a strange clinking noise when I entered). He stole a cup of soup from a nearby grocery store buffet, and he was at the end of his rope.

I asked him if he had friends, family, or any help in the area. He said he did. Some of those bridges burned long ago, but others, while in tatters, were possible options.

I've always been a big believer in getting people equipped and resourced with what they may need, so after asking a few questions to understand what this young man may need and what kinds of services I could get to him, I told him this: "You have no idea who you are talking to tonight. You asked if I believe in God, and you are asking for help. I want you to know who I am. I am a priest. I am the person God has sent to you to confirm His love for you. You are calling out to God, and He sent me.

"I never come to this theater," I continued (it was a "dollar" theater near our home that we seldom visit because they only ever show rom-coms, yuck). "My wife and I had dinner and decided to wander around, which we never do. After going into a shop, which I had never been in, we decided to come to see a movie. I just happened to go to the bathroom at the time you were here. You called out to God; I guess He sent me. There is literally no other reason for me to be here."

I prayed that God would continue to reveal his love and mercy to this young man. I prayed he would have the courage to reach out to friends for help, not just for tonight but to make a huge life change. I prayed for protection for him and uncommon wisdom.

When we finished, I asked if I could give him a ride anywhere or if he needed anything else from me. He said no, but he was grateful to have met me. We left the restroom together, and I watched him disappear into the dark Phoenix evening.

I don't remember what movie we went to. I don't know what I had for dinner. I don't know what I did when I got home, but I do remember how easily the tears came as I sat there thinking about that young man and the painful realization that he was facing a terrible uphill battle. Despite my best efforts and what I believe to be God directly intervening in his life, I have no idea how things turned out.

That's one funny thing about dignity—you don't always see the results.

Dignity lies in the DNA of every human being. There has never been a person, in the history of all humanity, who did not possess dignity. It is universal. Dignity is the unknown guest at every meal. It is the unseen force in every human interaction. It is the power to generate healing and to cause a life to change course. We know when it is validated and when it is violated.

Dignity is the unknown guest at every meal. It is the unseen force in every human interaction. It is the power to generate healing and to cause a life to change course.

Dignity is at the very core of what it means to be human. I possess it. You possess it. The homeless, drug-addicted guy in a random theater bathroom possesses it. The question is: What do we do about it?

Entering Stories: The Veteran

I want to tell you about Spike. Actually, his name is Neil, and he wears a Vietnam veteran hat. I noticed his hat as I walked through the produce section of our local grocery store. I waited to get closer to him before I said anything, and when he was close enough, I extended my hand and told him, "Thank you for serving."

He smiled and said, "It was my pleasure."

I asked him when he served and with which branch. He was in the Air Force, helping get planes and choppers ready to go, carrying supplies, ammo, and soldiers to needed areas. Recently, I was told that a helicopter required three hours of work for every hour of operation to ensure its safety. While I don't know the details, I know those who work on the machines and vehicles are every bit as important as anyone in them. I've often heard how the "Air Force guys" saved the necks of those on the ground in Vietnam. They played a vital role.

Spike played a critical role and sacrificed much. I know war, of any kind or duration, requires people to give in ways no one can really count. Oftentimes, the soldiers themselves have memories and emotions that prove difficult to address. Once they transition to civilian life, many find it nearly impossible, and some decide it is simply too much. There is a loss of identity, purpose, and comradery that leaves a void for the rest of their lives. But that's just the surface.

The loved ones of service members pay a heavy price. Spouses, children, and others spend weeks and months wondering if they will have to live without those they love and cherish. And sometimes, when the service members do come home, they have changed. War does that. It changes people. You simply can't be who you were when you left.

Sometimes the price paid is physical. Service members return home and have to adapt to life with a disability. Maybe it's a head injury, or they have to learn to navigate life with prosthetics. Maybe it's hearing loss or the effects of Agent Orange on the limbs and in hearts like it is with my dad. Those caring for servicemen and women suffer along with them, watching them struggle and fight to regain some semblance of normality.

Perhaps more profound is the emotional price they pay. Post-traumatic stress disorder (PTSD) affects many. Dreams, memories, nightmares, sudden rages, or overflowing tears can come at any moment and leave everyone in their wake. The shame and guilt people carry require tremendous courage and strength to unpack. If not PTSD, survivor's guilt can also stop service members in their tracks. Memorial Day is the worst day for many, not for what they lost but because they came home. Serving in the military comes at a great cost for the soldier and their loved ones.

I watched Spike as he told me about his duties and the experiences he had. He told me about his friends who didn't make it and about the ones who did make it, only to come home and find they had no life in the U.S.

Finally, his eyes began to water, and his voice cracked as he said these words: "Make sure you tell your dad: Welcome Home." It was Spike's experience, as well as my dad's, that homecoming produced another set of issues. Instead of coming home to a hero's welcome, they were greeted with protesters. The uniform they wore with pride as they got off the plane became a scarlet letter. They couldn't get out of them fast enough. Spike said he was called names, terrible names, that made no sense to him. He hadn't done any of the things he was accused of. He tried to serve his country with honor the same way many he knew had done in Korea and WWII. My dad's welcome home included spit from a protester at the airport in San Francisco. The tears spilled out of Spike's eyes, right there in the grocery store. Despite his strong exterior, even after nearly fifty years, he could still feel the pain. He accepted the hug I gave him but with a quick ending and an intense effort to re-gather himself.

I told him how much I appreciated him sharing with me. I was grateful for him finding love again after his wife of thirty-four years had died. I was thankful for his kids and his eight grandkids who bring him life. Through my own moist eyes, I told Neil that he was loved.

We parted ways after what was a 20-minute interaction, grateful for each other, appreciative of making a connection that went so deep so quickly. Both of us changed a little. When I got home, I interrupted my dad who was watching TV to tell him my story about Spike. He listened carefully and was moved when I told him that Spike told me to tell him "Welcome Home." Common experiences, even though they may be as terrible as war and its subsequent results can be a pathway for dignity.

Entering Stories: Injured
Recently, while leaving a store with a friend, we encountered a strange scene. A man was stumbling about the parking lot while another older gentleman intentionally stepped in front of him in some awkward dance.

"Should I call 911?" a woman nearby asked.

"What happened?" I asked.

"This man ran into several cars in the parking lot and even into the building!" She replied. I told her she should call 911 as I brought my attention back to the weird dance the two men were performing.

The older man produced a badge and mentioned something about the sheriff's office while trying to stay before the staggering man.

As I sized up the situation, I knew I had a couple of options to choose from. The older gentleman was getting ready to fight. He said the stumbling man was getting "froggy." I could join him in the escalation, though I'm not sure either wanted to fight, especially the stumbling, apparently drunk man. It would have been easy to take him to the ground and pin his arms behind his back while we waited for the police. I may have taken a bump or a bruise, but it was an option.

My other choice was to de-escalate. I told the older man, "I got you." I wanted him to know that if anything physical happened, I would intervene. I repeated this to him about every thirty seconds while he danced with the drunk man. My presence and comments had a calming effect on him as he slowly calmed down and stopped dancing.

I turned my attention to the drunk man (though I was still not sure what substance was influencing his behavior). He stepped towards me, then backward and occasionally side to side.

"How's your day going?" I asked him.

"I am having a hard time with my balance," he said.

That much was obvious.

"I'm sorry to see that. What's your name?"

"Jefferson."

"Where are you from, Jefferson?"

"I am from here?"

"All your life?"

"Yep, we moved here a while ago," further indicating the depths of his intoxication.

He was young, looked solid and broad-shouldered, but incredibly sad.

"Why are you having trouble with your balance?" I asked.

"I fell off a platform in 2008. I was working when the ladder slipped out from under me, and I fell and hit my head." He explained the story with motions and sound effects.

"I am so sorry," I said. "Have things been hard since then?"

He told me how things had been difficult, how he couldn't keep a job because of the effects of the fall. Thankfully, he wasn't belligerent or violent. He clearly didn't know what he'd done. Like many with injury, chronic pain, and loss of ability, I surmised that he turned to alcohol to numb the pain. Instead of seeing a drunk trying to flee the scene of an accident, I saw a guy whose life was turned upside down by accident. How many people have I known like that? How many times have I personally whistled past that graveyard myself?

I listened patiently as we leaned on a nearby vehicle. In the meantime, the police arrived and began talking with the older gentleman. I told Jefferson the police were going to want to chat with him as they respectfully approached.

I had a choice to make at that moment, and I am glad I chose to talk with Jefferson. I could have told a story about a takedown, struggle, and custody and control. Instead, I'm far happier with making a connection with him, however brief and broken it may have been. It reminds me of the quote: "Everyone you meet is fighting a battle you know nothing about. Be kind. Always."

People are stories, and we don't know in which chapter we are meeting them. Are we encountering them at the end, middle, or beginning of their story? Are we playing a role in their story? If we are, what character do we want to be? Sometimes we get to choose which role we play; I got to choose which role I played with Jefferson. At other times, the roles may be decided for us, so how we play our roles is up to us. Conversely, we need to consider what role the other person is playing in *our* story? Where have they intersected with us? How we relate to them still matters.

That is how dignity works. When we recognize it in another person, we have the opportunity to validate it. It is always there for the seeing. When we do, something beautiful happens, and humanity becomes more than another species wandering the earth. We are ennobled. We are honored, and we know on a deep level that we matter: the dignity carrier and the dignity validator.

It can happen in the movies, a grocery store over some produce, or in a parking lot.

With us and in us, that's how dignity's power grows and how dignity wins.

CHAPTER 13
An Ancient Power
Dignity is Not a New Idea

I**T IS EASY TO** think of dignity as a new idea, something born through humanity's advancement and evolution in its thinking about self and community. But the ancients, while not perfect, had a profound sense of the meaning and value of every human being.

Author David Bentley Hart argues that it was as early as the first century that "our modern notion that there is such a thing as innate human worth, residing in every individual of every class and culture, is at best the very late consequence of a cultural, conceptual, and moral revolution that erupted many centuries earlier, and in the middle of a world that was anything but hospitable to its principles."[26]

---

26 – David Bentley Hart, "Human Dignity Was a Rarity Before Christianity," Church Life Journal, October 17, 2017, https://churchlifejournal.nd.edu/articles/human-dignity-was-a-rarity-before-christianity.

In recent history, there are people who have validated the dignity of others, unleashing its power in beautiful ways. Looking back gives us an opportunity to do it like they did, though in some cases, it seems far beyond the average person's ability. Mother Theresa's work with the poor in India, Martin Luther King Jr.'s leadership during the Civil Rights Movement in the 1960s, and the fight against apartheid in South Africa led by Nelson Mandela feel out of reach for most of us. These are simply amazing people in extraordinary circumstances who made beautiful choices. It is easy to put them on a pedestal and point and say, "Be like them."

It is beneficial to strive after those we admire. As such, I want to posit another example.

There are always numerous reactions when people bring up Jesus. Some get excited, some look exhausted, some roll their eyes, others sigh heavily—maybe even a few of these at the same time. And now with the mention of his name, maybe you're even considering skipping this section of the book.

Stick with me here. I use Jesus here as an example of someone who, in an unremarkable way, validated someone's dignity and to show the profound change that occurred in that person's when he did. I encourage you to read the following story through the lens of dignity and see if it isn't something that you and I can emulate.

The Story of a Little Man

Zacchaeus was an unusual young man. He was little for his age. His head appeared a bit too large for his body and his limbs too short. His fingers were too tiny for his hands. Today, we would call Zacchaeus a dwarf or a little person. Back then, he was an embarrassment. Zacchaeus grew up in an area and a time when these kinds of things produced shame.

When a child like Zacchaeus was born, the assumption was that the parents did something wrong. It was their fault; they were sinful people. There had to be something wrong with them or their family for God to allow a baby like this to be born. God was behind everything.

This belief followed Zacchaeus and his family as he grew. Imagine how that might have haunted them at work or him in school. There was subtle and not-so-subtle judgment in their eyes. There were whispers and maybe even laughter as he tried to deal with everyday life as a little person. He was a derision. Aberrant. He and his family bore the shame and guilt of it every single day.

Bitterness likely grew in his heart and mind as he aged. Everywhere he went, whatever he did, he was reminded of his status. He was less-than.

When Rome invaded his country, things became interesting. The army took over the region and put a boot on the chin of Zacchaeus' people. They were merciless, executing people they thought were traitors and imposing taxes on the conquered to pay for the privilege to live under their rule. Conquered? Pay up!

Even worse, they chose a local, one of the defeated, to collect taxes—double the insult. To add insult to injury, the Romans chose someone the people scorned. They chose someone hard to respect. To ensure the conquered people were kept in their place, they chose Zacchaeus to collect their taxes.

For the people, this was a reminder of who was really in charge. It wasn't them. The sinful one, whom God despised, whom God had forsaken, got to take their money. Maybe God had abandoned them?

For Zacchaeus, it was a chance to make a good living. Perhaps not just a good living, but a great one. All he had to do was pledge allegiance to his enemy, which might not have been a difficult choice because his people treated him poorly already.

Zacchaeus became the chief tax collector, meaning he benefited greatly. For each tax collected, he took a little for himself, paying everyone back for the difficulty he experienced in their community. He soon became very wealthy and powerful off the region's trade. This arrangement went on for some time, with his wealth growing each passing day until it all came to a head at a single dinner party.

Rumors amidst the crowds swirled about a new teacher in the area. He was causing a great deal of controversy in the things he said and did. He talked with women he shouldn't. He hung out with people of little character. Some even said he healed people.

His name was Jesus, and by this time, everyone in the region knew about him, or at least thought they did. He was on the radar of the Roman oppressors and the Jewish leaders. Rome watched him closely as he had the makings of a rebel and revolutionary. Was he going to lead a violent revolt? Was he going to challenge the Emperor's authority? Was he going to disturb the Pax Romana? The Jewish leaders watched him with even more scrutiny. They seemed to be in his crosshairs often. His teaching was pointed and critical of them. He did things that flaunted their rules and made them out to be hypocrites. He was someone people wanted to see, hear, touch, and be around.

When Jesus came through Zacchaeus' town, Zacchaeus wanted to see what all the fuss was about. Even though it would bring more scorn and wasn't what a socially respectable person would do, because of his size, Zacchaeus climbed a tree.

Here is how the Gospel of Luke records it: "He [Jesus] entered Jericho and was passing through. And behold, there was a man named Zacchaeus. He was a chief tax collector and was rich. And he was seeking to see who Jesus was, but on account of the crowd he could not, because he was small in stature. So he ran on ahead and climbed up into a sycamore tree to see him, for he was about to pass that way" (Luke 19:1–4).

Then an interesting thing happened: Jesus noticed Zacchaeus. Of all the people in the whole crowd from the entire town clamoring for his attention, he stopped at Zacchaeus. Maybe Zacchaeus was easy to spot in the tree, and maybe it was even a bit humorous to see a wealthy man perched there, but Jesus noticed Zacchaeus in a way the others did not. The author Luke does not record that Jesus had never met Zacchaeus or had any dealings with him prior to this moment, still Jesus sees him and calls him by name. "And when Jesus came to the place, he looked up and said to him, 'Zacchaeus, hurry and come down, for I must stay at your house today'" (verse 5).

Now, if you spent any time in church or sat in a Sunday school lesson as a child, you might have heard this song:

Zacchaeus was a wee little man
And a wee little man was he
He climbed up in a sycamore tree
For the Lord he wanted to see

And when the Savior passed that way
He looked up in the tree
And said, "Zacchaeus, you come down!
For I'm going to your house today!
For I'm going to your house today!"

Zacchaeus was a wee little man
But a happy man was he
For he had seen the Lord that day
And a happy man was he;
And a very happy man was he.

I don't know who wrote this song, and I'm not sure why we teach it to kids this way, but the section that says, "Zacchaeus, you come down," is nearly always interpreted as Jesus being angry with Zacchaeus as the hand motions in this part of the song include a hand on one hip and finger pointing upward and wagging at Zacchaeus. Maybe a frazzled Sunday school teacher wrote the song and interpreted the story this way.

I think that's the wrong interpretation though.

In speaking directly to Zacchaeus, Jesus was not rebuking him but inviting him: "I want to dine with you, Zacchaeus. I want to spend time with you, Zacchaeus. I want to be in your presence. Come down so I can be with you."

Imagine being the center of attention like that. The whole town is there, and when Jesus sees Zacchaeus in the tree, he stops not to chide but to bless. He didn't stop to make fun of him, talk bad about him, or make a point of him. Instead, Jesus stopped and gave him a great gift. He validated Zacchaeus' dignity, and he did so in front of everyone.

How did Zacchaeus respond? "So he hurried and came down and received him joyfully" (verse 6). Zacchaeus is excited and full of joy that Jesus would do this for him.

How does the crowd respond? "And when they saw it, they all grumbled, 'He has gone in
to be the guest of a man who is a sinner'" (verse 7).

Jesus can't be that great if he entertains spending time with a tax collector, let alone Zacchaeus! They can't believe that this teacher, this great prophet, and possibly Israel's Messiah would bother to attend to someone like Zacchaeus. Zacchaeus doesn't deserve it; he betrayed his people, defrauded them, and lived the life of a rich man!

Isn't it funny how some people react to dignity being validated in others?

But Zacchaeus got it. He fully embraced what Jesus did for him. It was as if by those simple actions and words, his life was transformed. Indeed, that is what Luke wrote: "And Zacchaeus stood and said to the Lord, 'Behold, Lord, the half of my goods I give to the poor. And if I have defrauded anyone of anything, I restore it fourfold.' And Jesus said to him, 'Today salvation has come to this house, since he also is a son of Abraham. For the Son of Man came to seek and to save the lost'" (verses 8–10).

Zacchaeus' salvation came through dignity. Jesus didn't tell him how sinful he was. He didn't point out his eternal destiny. He didn't make him pray. Instead, Jesus treated Zacchaeus with dignity. This somehow led to his transformation.

Would the people around you might benefit from you doing the same? If we allow Jesus and the Scriptures to be a model, we have a chance at living lives that reflect what He is like.

Genesis teaches that man is made in God's image. God placed man in the temple He created (earth) to reflect his image to the world he made:[27] "Then God said, 'Let us make man in our image, after our likeness. And let them have dominion over the fish of the sea and over the birds of the heavens and over the livestock and over all the earth and over every creeping thing that creeps on the earth.' So God created man in his own image, in the image of God he created him; male and female he created them" (Genesis 1:26–27).

To be fully human means to embody and reflect God's image to a world deprived of it. That is what Jesus did, so if you want to know what God is like, look at Jesus.

Our "job" is to embrace our identity and validate the identity of those around us, namely as being people created in the image of our Creator. Despite status, wealth, skin color, sexual orientation, addiction, religion, or political affiliation, every single human being bears the image of God. Every. Single. One. Even that coworker you don't like, or the person who cut you off in traffic. From the most revered to the most despised. Everyone bears the image of God and is therefore of inestimable worth.

---

27 – John H. Walton, *The Lost World of Genesis One: Ancient Cosmology and the Origins Debate* (Downers Grove, IL: IVP Academic, 2009).

In short, all have dignity.

Whether they know it or not, whether they act like it or not, or whether you think they deserve it or not, it is true for everyone. That is one of the most compelling things about Jesus: He treated everyone with dignity. The people on the fringes, the lepers, the blind, the beggars, the poor, the bloody, those who were full of shame and guilt are the ones he interacted with. He talked to them. He touched them. He defended them.

Why would people who were the lowest of the low in society, the prostitutes, tax collectors, drunkards, and the "sinners," want to hang out with the holiest man who ever lived? Most of the time, when I am around holy people, I feel a bit awkward. I am acutely aware of how unholy I am. I haven't done what Mother Theresa has done. I've not dedicated my life to living in a monastery hovering over the Scriptures and cultivating my spiritual life. I have a hard time not cussing, let alone being described as holy. What was it about Jesus? It's simple. He didn't treat them according to their actions but according to their identity. He treated them like they were image bearers. He didn't make objects out of them. He validated their dignity. That is why they wanted to be around him. He made them feel human. There was no prerequisite for treatment with dignity. If there was, it was shame and guilt, because they all had it (we all have it) in spades.

Zacchaeus at Work

Our workplaces are full of people who have experienced pain and derision like Zacchaeus. They've been ostracized and had their dignity violated. They may not even realize how precious they are. They may have no way of knowing their true identity; they may only define themselves by their work. The only time they may have felt value is if they've contributed to the bottom line. But it doesn't have to be this way.

An example of dignity from my world is from my friend Jay Pages. Jay is my Brazilian Jiu-Jitsu instructor at Jay Pages Jiu-Jitsu Academy in Tempe, Arizona. He is kind and generous, and excellent at what he does. He and his wife Lisa (who is no less kind or deadly) married fifteen years ago. When they did, Jay partnered with Lisa to raise her daughter Celissa. Throughout the years, he was a loving and devoted dad. Jay did his best to be present and support Celissa in all she did.

He was her dad in every way but one—on paper. Jay wanted to adopt Celissa for the longest time, but it wasn't possible until recently. Celissa turned eighteen, and unbeknownst to Jay, had all the official adoption paperwork completed. She wanted Jay to be her dad, not just in her heart but on paper. All that was required was a signature.

For Jay's birthday, she presented him with a manila envelope. He curiously opened it to find everything filed and ready to go. It was official, and the internet officially broke. His response and the response of the family have been viewed over 58 million times!

Why the reaction? It is an incredible video, to be sure, but it's something more. It gets to our core. It speaks to a longing in our hearts and minds. It speaks of dignity. When dignity is validated, we know it. We can smell it. We cherish it. We celebrate it. It restores our faith in humanity.

There are glimpses of dignity on display these days, and we must be the kind of people to promote them. Glimpses and flashes of beauty help us realize there is more to the world than the machines and structures that make society "go." They give us hope that people really matter and that we are more than just numbers and bottom lines.

Now, when it comes to validating the dignity others posess, of the utmost importance is to recognize the dignity *we* possess. This can be a difficult proposition; it is often easier to see it and protect it and defend it in others. But our gaze must shift to the mirror. Being a dignity champion and unleashing its power in and through us means we see it and celebrate it in ourselves. The next chapter will help us take steps in that direction.

CHAPTER 14
Obstacles to Embracing our Dignity
The Difficulty of Validating Our Own Dignity

YOU PROBABLY KNOW THE adage "pain is a great teacher." Most people have encountered pain, some even tremendous pain. It is part of the human experience. Now, if it's true that pain is a great teacher, wouldn't there be more PhDs among us? Unfortunately, that's not how pain works.

Dealing with grief and pain is not something we are usually keen on processing. Rather than learning coping skills, identifying our emotions, and knowing what to do with them, it's easier to set it all aside or sweep under that big rug. It's easier to lash out than walk through the feelings. Pain hurts and grief is hard, so the instant gratification we get from shoving a painful experience far from us works. We don't feel the pain anymore.

Stuffing it, pushing it away, or using other avoidance tactics make sense, but only at the time. How we handle our suffering and pain says a lot about how we value and validate our dignity.

The Problem of Pain

The problem is, when we avoid pain, we only shelve it for a later date. It can become a habit: We encounter another painful episode or experience grief again and we remember the shelved pain, so we walk out to the garage, make more room on the shelf, and place the fresh pain and grief alongside the others. After a while though, the pain begins to leak out, and maybe we don't notice that all the contents have leaked onto the floor. Then every time we set new emotions on the shelf, we step in the old and take them with us. Eventually, any negative emotion, big or small, can unleash an entire garage full of unprocessed grief and pain. What on the surface looks like no big deal triggers an avalanche of pain. And on it goes, burying relationships that unwittingly encounter the emotional time bomb.

If pain is such a great teacher, wouldn't it help us to easily navigate our emotions when hurt? Pain isn't a great teacher, though it is a tool that can teach us things and help us grow. While unpleasant, pain doesn't have to stop us dead in our tracks or be regulated to a storage area just waiting to spill out or explode onto everyone and everything.

One challenge to effectively using this useful tool is our pace. We don't allow the pain process to slow down. The infliction of pain can happen fast, and we fail to recognize the pain as the primary experience.

Anger, for instance, is a secondary emotion, masking the pain we feel, but in the moment of the pain being served, anger is the emotion many tend to run with. In our anger, we say and do things we regret. In our anger, we blame and lash out to deal with the pain we feel. Anger is simply a mask. When someone wears the mask of anger, it can generally be assumed they are in a great deal of pain and may be unsure how to deal with it (not to mention how some will choose to destroy the person or thing that causes the pain).

Distancing ourselves from pain can be helpful to give us time and space to address it, but "killing" our pain and stuffing it in the garage only results in the need to do so every time we experience it. A singularly ineffective way of being genuinely human is being ready for violence any time you are hurt. We are not unlike other animals that when wounded, lash out or bite another. We can also lash out at well-intentioned people who are trying to help.

When was the last time you got angry? What made you that way? Can you recognize that it originated in the pain you experienced?

The Process

Once you can see the pain clearly, you have some choices to make: You can get help treating your pain; you can self-treat the pain; or you can equip yourself with tools to help you deal with pain when it comes your way.

Maybe you are accustomed to self-treating, which is what created a leaky garage filled with toxic emotions that feel less and less containable. Or you've successfully found a way to push pain and grief aside (for the time being), feeling "successful" with your efforts.

If "everything is ok" or "it's not that big of a deal" are words you say when hurt, you should be aware that you may not be walking through your pain. You may be avoiding it by setting it aside. So, if this is not a helpful way of processing pain, what steps can we take to address it?

Acknowledge the Hurt

Did you know the brain processes physical pain and emotional pain in the same location? Emotional pain and physical pain are both genuine and have significant consequences. "Sticks and stones may break my bones, but names will never hurt me" is an unfortunate lie we tell ourselves to avoid the pain we feel when others belittle us or violate our dignity.

Imagine someone with a broken leg who doesn't believe it's broken, despite its noticeable misalignment. Not acknowledging a broken leg has a number of serious ramifications: You will encounter immediate and long-term pain and immediate and long-term disability; you'll experience peripheral alignment issues as your body attempts to compensate for the injured limb; and you may encounter infection, loss of the limb itself, and possibly even death.

Without being too dramatic, not treating our emotional pain and wounding has the same effect. We emotionally limp and wince whenever we're reminded of the incident or person who caused us the pain. To avoid more pain and grief, we use other methods to compensate, still making our wounding our primary experience. We fear the pain lasting, growing worse, or happening again, so we orient our lives around avoiding it at all costs. We do this by avoiding certain people, situations, or conversations. This leads to a death within us as well as death to our relationships.

C. S. Lewis said, "Mental pain is less dramatic than physical pain, but it is more common and also more hard to bear. The frequent attempt to conceal mental pain increases the burden. It is easier to say 'My tooth is aching' than to say 'My heart is broken.'"

Acknowledging the hurt and pain we feel, and the grief we bear is an essential first step.

Learn to Separate Pain and Thoughts

Another critical step toward walking through and with your pain is learning how to separate your pain and your thoughts. For many of us, our thoughts and emotions live in the same space, and the entanglement makes it difficult to untangle one from the other. Did the thought lead to the feeling, or did the feeling lead to the thought? Did the situation trigger the thought? Was the resulting action based on the circumstance or the feeling?

While challenging, deciphering our thoughts from our emotions allows us to slow the pain and grief process down so we can examine and clean the wound, preparing it for treatment.

To help people walk with integrity in their faith, first-century writer Paul encouraged his readers to "take every thought captive," meaning to literally examine their thoughts. Learning how to enter into and practice this skill of examining one's thoughts will help with pain and grief and keep us from being enslaved to our emotions. Today, this is called practicing mindfulness.

I've experienced migraines for as long as I can remember. The medical profession still doesn't understand all the ins and outs of what they are, why they happen, and how to treat them. Because of this, I have been poked, prodded, tested, analyzed, and experimented upon in order to try to find relief. Little helps the physical pain of migraines for me so we try to limit the symptoms. A few years ago, after a particularly long cycle of pain and suffering, I was depressed. The physical pain took a significant emotional toll and I found myself in a therapist's office.

He asked me a key question: "Can you tell me about your relationship with migraines?"

Initially, I had no words. My relationship with my headaches? Seriously? What are you talking about?

But after a moment of considering his question, the words came swiftly: "I hate them. They rob everything from me! If they were a person, I would have killed them a long time ago!"

"So, you would say you have a negative relationship with your headaches?" he asked.

"Are you kidding me? Of course, I do!"

And so began my journey of mindfulness, taking every thought captive when it came to my headaches. Validating my dignity in the midst of physical and emotional pain proved to be one of the most important things I've ever done. I learned the skill of separating my thoughts from my emotions. I learned to think about my migraines without all the shame and guilt piling on me. I began to accept the migraines and even welcome them when they came instead of clenching my teeth, balling up my fists, and digging in my heels. It wasn't easy and is still difficult. This validates my dignity by helping me to see I am more than my thoughts. I am not just how my migraines makes me feel. I am not a helpless victim of my biology. I can evaluate my thinking and make choices about what I spend time ruminating on. Because of this, my identity isn't wrapped up in my depression or pain, but in my fundamental acknowledgment of my worth.

More Than Our Circumstances

This change didn't happen overnight. It was easy for me to see the dignity in those around me but hard to acknowledge it in myself. How I saw myself was different from the reality of who I was. I was loved, cherished, cared for, and valuable to my family, though I couldn't feel or believe it because of the guilt and shame I carried. Taking control of my thoughts about migraines, how they made me feel, how my family thought about me, and how I thought about myself was incredibly powerful. I was no longer a slave to my mind. I was freed to value the thoughts that came to mind or allow them to pass without much notice. Once I was unencumbered by thoughts and emotions, I was able to be more present to myself and my family. It was a game-changer. Instead of feeling violated and victimized, I could accept what was happening to me. Instead of being angry, I could feel sad. Instead of being crippled, I had power over my life.

I've recognized other areas of my life in which practicing this skill has led to more freedom and a greater degree of resilience. In fact, when helping leaders develop strength, I start with dignity because dignity is at the heart of resilience. Validating the dignity you possess means you accept your value and importance even in the face of an inability to perform or produce. Dignity pushes back against the forces that would define us by "worthless" means. You are not defined by your work. You are not what you do. You are more than that. Everyone is.

Life can be incredibly hard. Circumstances can bring us to our knees and make us wonder: Why is this happening to me? Why did this person do this? Why is my job so hard? Why, why, why?

There are answers to the why question, but they are generally mundane and less than helpful.

For instance, why do people get cancer? Cells change in our bodies sometimes from outside sources, chemicals exposure, or lifestyle choices we make. Other times it's genetic and passed down from generations to visit you.

Why does genocide happen? It has to do with how people orient themselves to power and whom they blame for situations they face.

Why do people get bullied? In a small way, it is the same as genocide. If we can objectify someone, we can treat them any way we like.

You get my drift. There are reasons things happen, but the answers seldom give us a sense of peace or hope when facing them. On the contrary, they can add salt to the wound by providing our "reasons" for what happens. Instead, what people want to know is that they matter and what is happening to them matters. They often want to know someone is with them in the pain and the suffering. They want to know they are not alone.

It is easy to look at our circumstances to find our worth. When things are good and lined up as we would like, we believe we are doing well. We think we're good, and it is easy to believe our lives have worth and meaning. But when dignity isn't our center, we are tempted to believe we are only as good, valuable, or worthy as our circumstances tell us.

It isn't unlike the ancients who looked to the natural world to tell them how their gods felt about them. When the volcano erupted, the gods were angry. When the mountain was quiet, all was well. If it rained, the gods were happy, crops grew, and there was an abundant harvest. If it rained too much, there was a flood, and the gods were angry, wiping out the farmers' hard work. If it didn't rain at all, the results were the same.

Our circumstances cannot and do not tell us our worth. Various things happen to us in life, and when we view life as our enemy, we view ourselves as hapless victims. Others then determine the trajectory of our lives and what happens to us. We are unable to do anything but endure the terrors life visits upon us.

This outlook creates a negative view of life, not only for us but for others. We have limited impact and influence for good when we determine that everything is out of our control or that we are at the whim of great malevolence.

Life Is My Friend

When life is my friend, it leads to dignity. If our circumstances do not define us, we can honor and embrace our own dignity.

Recently, I watched a program where two men decided to ride their motorcycles around the globe. They frequently faced challenges, but none was more significant than what happened in the furthest part of northeast Asia. In the middle of nowhere, their bikes broke down, and with seemingly no way to forward, they persevered. They could have tried a more accessible road but would have missed out on what lay ahead. They could have quit but would have regretted it the rest of their lives. Instead, they decided to press on and press in. Watching them figure out new ways to use tools, leveraging relationships with locals, or being ingenious with encouragement was inspiring. It was never "we can't"; it was always "how are we going to do this?"

It's a vastly different way of approaching life. When life is your friend, circumstances become gifts, no matter how difficult they are.

From Viktor Frankl:

> This young woman knew that she would die in the next few days. But when I talked to her, she was cheerful in spite of this knowledge. "I am grateful that fate has hit me so hard," she told me. "In my former life, I was spoiled and did not take spiritual accomplishments seriously." Pointing through the window of the hut, she said, "This tree here is the only friend I have in my loneliness." Through that window she could see just one branch of a chestnut tree, and on the branch were two blossoms. "I often talk to this tree," she said to me.
>
> I was startled and didn't quite know how to take her words. Was she delirious? Did she have occasional hallucinations? Anxiously I asked her if the tree replied. "Yes." What did it say to her? She answered,

"It said to me, 'I am here, I am here, I am life, eternal life.'"[28]

The extraordinary capacity for humans to shift their mindset and view circumstances as a friend versus foe makes for hope and an unshakable affirmation of our dignity. When life is our friend, we believe that we can do things, we can accomplish tasks. We are worthy. We are valuable. We are powerful. We can figure it out. We can.

We are not victims. We aren't helpless. We aren't painfully floating through the universe at the whim of whatever may happen. We are important, we matter, and we have value. Our lives have meaning. It is never a question of *if* we can do something; it is *how we will do it*.

Look at Nic Vujicic:

> Nick Vujicic ("voo-Yi-chich") is an Australian-American born without arms or legs. He has become a world-renowned speaker, *New York Times* best-selling author, coach, and entrepreneur.
>
> Nick faced tremendous obstacles in life, from living life without limbs to being bullied at school and fearful for his future with no purpose in sight. Without hope, his feelings of helplessness and isolation led him to attempt suicide. Nick persevered through life's challenges and discovered fundamental principles which enabled him to find his purpose and turn obstacles into opportunities, making him one of

---

28 – Viktor Emil Frankl, *Man's Search for Meaning: An Introduction to Logotherapy* (Boston: Beacon Press, 1959), pg 90.

the most sought-after keynote speakers in the world! Millions of people have found hope, purpose, and the strength to overcome their challenges through Nick's inspirational speeches and powerful coaching.

Nick is an anti-bullying advocate who travels the globe speaking to millions of students in partnership with several governments' Education Departments. Nick has created an innovative Social Emotional Learning (SEL) Curriculum called "Attitude Is Altitude," wherein he teaches students to make positive changes in their lives and their communities.[29]

Nick is extraordinary in every way. When we see what he deals with daily and what he is overcoming, we believe that the problems we face (which are likely far less intense) can be overcome. We don't ask *if* but we ask *how*. We realize we *can*. Nick's life and his outlook help us see that there are ways we can overcome what we are facing.

At the fundamental level, Nick embraces his dignity. He embraces his dignity by having a positive impact and influencing others in a meaningful way. His circumstances define him only as a reference point. He is no victim.

Accepting what is and creatively thinking of ways to move forward is critical when we think of our own dignity. When we accept what is as a reference point and not a definition, we give ourselves a chance to write a different story over our lives. Our challenging circumstances become tunnels, not pits, taking us from point A to point B. They

---

29 – Nick Vujicic, accessed November 12, 2022, https://nickvujicic.com.

are dark and complex but take us from where we were to where we want to be.

In embracing our dignity, we find hope and meaning, and strangely enough, we help others with their dignity. Our lives are on display in one form or another. Family, friends, co-workers, and others are watching us, and they take notice. It may be little things, and you may never hear about how it happened, but people are taking cues from you. When you validate your own dignity, even in tough circumstances, you permit others to do the same with theirs. You may never have the chance to speak overtly about it, and you may never get to shout "dignity!" from the rooftops, but you will be doing so by your actions, and that matters.

Primary Identity

Dignity is about this primary identity. Fundamentally we have worth and value. You are valuable. You are worthy. You are important. How are these things true? What value do you possess?

You have value.

CEOs get large salaries because they bring leadership and value to the companies they serve. The companies believe the pay and benefits they offer are worth what they receive in return from the CEO. It is an exchange.

Google the net worth of any CEO or celebrity. The results show you how much money they have and equate it to their worth or their value. That is much of what our culture celebrates.

We perceive value in something or someone, so we are willing to exchange money or goods to get what we value. But what do we do when someone can no longer offer us what we think we need? We discard them, fire them, or stop calling. Sometimes we may find a better fit for them somewhere else so they can still be of some use. Either way, the focus is on what they can provide.

It makes sense...until it doesn't.

If the only way we view people is what they can provide us, we miss much. We are back to the objectification discussion. I am not saying you should do business with people who don't help you accomplish your goals or that you should hire people who can't do the required job. I am saying that their worth goes far beyond their capabilities.

"One man's trash is another man's treasure." Just because you can't find value in someone doesn't mean they hold no value. When someone is described as worthless, I always wonder *to whom?* Society? Your workspace? They aren't worthless to their friends. They aren't worthless to their families. In fact, the only place they may be "worthless" is to you and the small role they possess at work.

This chapter is about you and the dignity you possess, so turn your attention to yourself. Are you feeling worthless? Do you believe you are insignificant? Do you think you aren't of any value?

If we argue that people only have value based on their ability to produce, then we need to address some severe dilemmas. For instance, children cannot produce. When young, they eat, sleep, cry, and poop. They cost money and time. Are they an investment we expect a return on? By the production metric, children hold no value. The elderly or infirmed are in the same boat.

No sane person I know would argue that children and the elderly have no value. Thinking like that is dangerous, but we do it subtly, especially when we think we are supposed to be productive.

Ever had to spend time healing from surgery or recuperating from illness? Spending time on the couch or in bed can drive people crazy because they believe their only value lies in what they can *do*. But we are human beings, not human doings. What makes you valuable when you can't produce? You can and must place your value elsewhere.

What do you do when you don't fit? You have goals and desires you want to accomplish, and because we are social creatures, you need others to get them done. What do we do when someone doesn't "work," and what about when that someone is us?

Embracing the truth of our own dignity means we find our value beyond our work and production. It gives us the opportunity to see the world through new eyes. It may be helpful at this point to look beyond the North American context for a moment. The world doesn't view everything the way the West does. In fact, we in the west have much to learn from those around us. In the next chapter, we will look at some concepts from overseas that let us see dignity from a different lens and maybe gives us a deeper understanding of what worth we possess.

CHAPTER 15

The Dignity Connection
What We're All Looking For

HAVE YOU HEARD OF *ikagai*? In his article for positivepsychology.com, Dr. Jeffery Gaines describes ikagai as "a Japanese concept that combines the terms *iki*, meaning 'alive' or 'life,' and *gai*, meaning 'benefit' or 'worth.' When combined, these terms mean 'that which gives your life worth, meaning, or purpose.'"[30]

Ikigai believes everyone has a purpose and meaning which are found in the conjunction of several vital factors in life: what we love, what the world needs, what we can get paid to do, and what we are good at.

Pursuing our meaning and purpose is a dignity-filled exercise. When we know about ourselves this way, we can

---

30 – Jeffrey Gaines, Ph.D, "The Philosophy of Ikigai: 3 Examples About Finding Purpose," PositivePsychology.com, November 17, 2020, https://positivepsychology.com/ikigai.

operate in a way that holds our worth with intentionality. It could be that you need to understand some of these elements to see your worth.

Gaines makes a further distinction:

> It is important to note that ikigai does not typically refer only to one's personal purpose and fulfillment in life, without regard to others or society at large.
>
> Although it has had some historical shifts in meaning, ikigai has usually been cited as both a personal pursuit and one of benefit to others. In the end, ikigai brings meaning, purpose, and fulfillment to your life while also contributing to the good of others.
>
> Further, everyone has an ikigai – their particular intersection of passion, talent, and potential to benefit others. It is only a matter of finding it. The journey to ikigai might require time, deep self-reflection, and effort, but it is one we can all make.

We have worth because we are part of something bigger than ourselves. We are connected in interesting and exciting ways. Particularly in the West and specifically in North America, we like to think of ourselves as autonomous and free. Other cultures don't have this idea. Their sense of interconnectedness is strong and provides deep meaning and value in Japan and other areas of the world.

Dignity Connects Us

Online magazine, *Exploring Your Mind,* shared an article about the Zulu tribe in Africa.[31] The tribe has a unique way of expressing dignity to one another in their greetings. Instead of a simple "hello" or a "hey," they say something profound to one another. They use the word *sawubona*. "It literally means 'I see you, you are important to me and I value you.' It's a way to make the other person visible and to accept them as they are with their virtues, nuances, and flaws." That is amazing. What a beautiful way to greet people. It implies connectedness in a way our simple greetings lack. The article also says, "Sawubona: All my attention is with you. I see you and I allow myself to discover your needs, to see your fears, to identify your mistakes and accept them. I accept you for what you are, and you are part of me." Imagine how different our workplaces, fun spaces, and even our homes would look if we interacted this way? How would you feel if someone genuinely communicated this to you?

In our hyper-connected world, we are lonelier than ever. A 2018 study by Cigna points this fact out in rather stark figures. The survey was conducted with 20,000 U.S. adults ages 18 years and older:

- Nearly half of Americans report sometimes or always feeling alone (46 percent) or left out (47 percent).
- One in four Americans (27 percent) rarely or never feel as though there are people who really understand them.

---

31 – Valeria Sabater, "Sawubona: An African Tribe's Beautiful Greeting," Exploring your mind, accessed November 12, 2022, https://exploringyourmind.com/sawubona-african-tribe-greeting.

- Two in five Americans sometimes or always feel that their relationships are not meaningful (43 percent) and that they are isolated from others (43 percent).
- One in five people reports they rarely or never feel close to people (20 percent) or feel like there are people they can talk to (18 percent).
- Americans who live with others are less likely to be lonely (average loneliness score of 43.5) compared to those who live alone (46.4). However, this does not apply to single parents/guardians (average loneliness score of 48.2); even though they live with children, they are more likely to be lonely.
- Only around half of Americans (53 percent) have meaningful in-person social interactions, such as having an extended conversation with a friend or spending quality time with family on a daily basis.
- Generation Z (adults ages 18-22) is the loneliest generation and claims to be in worse health than older generations.
- Social media use alone is not a predictor of loneliness; respondents defined as very heavy users of social media have a loneliness score (43.5) that is not markedly different from the score of those who never use social media (41.7).[32]

---

32 – 2018 Cigna U.S. Loneliness Index, https://www.cigna.com/assets/docs/newsroom/loneliness-survey-2018-fact-sheet.pdf

It becomes terribly difficult to validate our own dignity when we are disconnected and lonely, and it becomes easier to believe things that aren't true about ourselves as we spin false narratives.

However, when connected to people who honor our dignity, our identity becomes more secure, and our worth more apparent.

Saying "sawubona" to another person recognizes their dignity but also says much about our own. You are the kind of person who recognizes others. You help them to feel valued and feel like they matter. They are a part of your world because you've invited them into your life. This greeting implies humility and vulnerability and doesn't lead people to prove themselves to one another.

Am I advocating for you to walk around and speak Zulu to everyone you meet? Maybe. But they won't have a clue what you're saying, and you could cause some pretty awkward moments in the boardroom or elsewhere.

Still, imagine the beautiful impact you can have on others if you give them your full attention. For example, how might your family or coworkers respond if you asked how they were and sincerely meant it? Part of validating your own dignity is to be the kind of person who recognizes it in those around you. It is tough to give something away that you don't possess yourself. The more you champion the dignity in others, the more they recognize it in you, and the more you will see it in the mirror.

The Zulu response to sawubona is *shiboka*. It means, "I exist for you." Again, pause and consider what that means. There is no identity without one another. The concepts of isolation and individuality we operate in by default are nearly impossible to the Zulu when addressing one another this way.

The Gacaca courts in Rwanda, specifically after the genocide of 1994, operated similarly. Originally, they were used to address minor disputes. People would gather in the gacaca, the short grass, in order to come together and solve grievances. They were designed for restorative justice, reminding people they are connected, and their village didn't just exist for themselves. They allowed people to come together as a community to address crimes, hear apologies, seek forgiveness, and restore the connection. While entirely foreign to us, it is another example of how addressing one another with dignity connects us and how, as connected people, we possess dignity.

You Are Not Your Mistakes

Recognizing your dignity means you are unwilling to label yourself with your last mistake. You're not an idiot, and you are not stupid. You are a human being who made a mistake. You are not the sum of your errors. You are not a problem to be solved or a product to be sold. You are worthy.

You are not your last success either. Accomplishments are fleeting. As high as we ride our last promotion, the last recognition we received, or any other achievement, the lows are just around the corner. It's like when someone relies on their stardom for too long and doesn't realize no one watches their movies anymore.

I watched an interview with a famous Major League Baseball umpire who was receiving recognition for a stellar career. The interviewer asked him what the most challenging call was to make in baseball. His reply was brilliant. "The next one," he answered. He understood that he was only as good as his next call. Living that way means you have to stay present, focused, and ready at all times. That is how he earned so much respect. Because respect is behavior-based and dignity is inherent worth, even the worst day of mistakes and blunders can't smudge your dignity. Those things may cause a lack of respect, but they can't touch your value.

It is often easier to do this with others because we can be our own worst critics. We can be incredibly hard on ourselves and say things to ourselves that we would never dream of saying to another person. Just as in our relationships with others, we need to divorce behavior from identity. We must separate action from inherent worth, and we have to do this when we consider ourselves.

We need to learn to bring our feelings in line with what is true. We will not always feel dignified, especially when we've responded poorly to our boss raising their voice to us or when our kids are acting out. On days when we are tired, bored, or angry, it is hard to experience our dignity. When we know we've blown it relationally with those closest to us, or we get rejected, our dignity seems frail and non-existent. Digging deep around the belief that we possess inherent worth means moving past our accomplishments, rejections, failures, and successes. We are more than these things. The hard work of self-leadership and living a principled life requires us to validate our own dignity.

Not sure if you get it? Practice this little exercise. Finish this sentence as it relates to your character: I am the kind of person who....

How do you describe yourself? Are you hardworking? Kind? An overcomer? Thoughtful? Selfish? Do you treat your friends and family well? Are you the kind of person who lives by a set of rules? If so, what are they? Do you repay kindness with evil?

How you think about yourself matters. For example, if you believe you are worthy of dignity and that you possess it simply because you exist, you are more likely to be the kind of person who validates the dignity of others.

Overcoming the challenge of validating the dignity in yourself is one of the most essential leadership principles you may ever face. Someone who knows and validates their own dignity is a formidable force. Opinions do not easily sway them. They are not afraid to be vulnerable and truth-telling. They influence others in positive ways and make meaningful contributions wherever they grow. It's the kind of person we want around us and the kind of person we want to become.

Whether you believe your dignity comes from thousands of years of evolutionary development and the need for hunters and gatherers to unify for safety and security, or you are a faith-filled person and believe you and every human being were made in the image of God (not that the two are mutually exclusive), dignity is the common trait held by every human being on earth. Whether instinctive or by design, our longing for social interaction connects us to something far bigger than ourselves that puts humans on the moon, creates beauty around us, ennobles us to care and love for one another, and live lives of impact and meaning. It doesn't matter if you are a CEO, a middle manager, a chef at Denny's, a work-at-home parent, rancher, or police officer, you matter because you are you, and when we embrace this principle and truth, the power of dignity is activated.

CHAPTER 16

A Call to Action

Empathy, Compassion, Civility, and Beyond

As a child, how many times did you hear "respect your elders"? Elders hold positions of authority. We are expected to do what was necessary to learn from them and respect their position as a teacher, another adult, or another person of principal importance.

The problem is many of those in authority (yesterday and today) are not worthy of respect. Their behavior doesn't command respect; in fact, it does the opposite. It then falls to us to respect the office or the position that person holds. We can respect managers, directors, C-suite executives, and others when their behavior is worthy of respect. However, when we learn their behavior is unethical, unkind, careless, rude, or immoral, their character comes into question and we find it difficult to listen to them. We lose respect.

According to Rosalind Wiseman, the founder of Cultures of Dignity, an organization working to shift how we look at the wellbeing of students, when students see people in authority acting in ways that causes a loss of respect, "they disengage from school when it happens to them or they disengage in whatever it is that they're doing when they have an adult who is doing this." [33] On the other hand, when a person of principal in our lives behaves admirably, we respect them. When leaders and people of influence treat people with dignity, it makes them feel valued and honored. This is true in the workplace, the classroom, and our homes. What we know and what studies have shown time and time again is that happy people perform better. My kids perform better in every way when they are treated with dignity. The kids in my classroom performed better when allowed to express themselves and feel heard. You have likely noticed how you perform better at work when those around you helped you feel understood and important.

> When leaders and people of influence treat people with dignity, it makes them feel valued and honored.

Without these things, we are like kids in the classroom—we disengage. This is such a problem that companies and organizations are doing all they can to measure

---

[33] – Rosalind Wiseman, "The unexpected key to student engagement? Dignity.," Big Think, accessed November 12, 2022, https://bigthink.com/the-present/dignity-student-engagement.

engagement because they know that engagement is vital for excellence. Treating people with dignity leads directly to engagement. When people feel heard, valued, connected, worthy, and important, they engage.

Author and former editor at *The Wall Street Journal*, Sam Walker writes: "It's also important to understand what engagement really is. Some companies try to measure it by asking employees to rate their 'satisfaction' on a five-point scale. But the threshold for feeling satisfied is pretty low—decent pay and reasonable hours might accomplish that for most people. Today's workers aren't truly engaged unless their jobs generate feelings of purpose and personal growth."[34]

Using Gallup Poll's research, Walker explains that Gallup uses engagement as a metric when rating business teams. He says engagement is

> a belief among employees that they're doing meaningful work in a climate that supports personal growth and development. Gallup and others have shown, over many years, that highly engaged teams have significantly lower turnover and higher productivity and profitability, among other things.
>
> Roughly a third of employees in the U.S. are highly engaged, Gallup found, but inside successful businesses that figure can run north of 68%. It's not surprising that many companies have started measuring internal engagement and tinkering with new perks and initiatives to juice their scores.

---

34 – Sam Walker, "The Economy's Last Best Hope: Superstar Middle Managers," WSJ, March 23, 2019, https://www.wsj.com/articles/the-economys-last-best-hope-superstar-middle-managers-11553313606.

Why all this talk about engagement?

Because it is about the people and not about the tasks. It isn't just about the pay or the incentives; it is about how a company makes you feel. Clifton and Harter share in their book, *The Manager*, "Organizational defects aren't failures in processes but failures in maximizing human potential."[35]

The point of Walker's article and Gallup's poll is that the middle manager is the most critical factor in successful teams. It isn't the star pupil. It isn't the CEO or general managers. It isn't the director or the dean. Illustrating the point I made early in this book: principled people behave in principal ways. When managers choose dignity and value their employees, they build a culture of trust and support where people can thrive. Helping workers maximize their full potential, not just in accomplishing their tasks, is part of the new work we must do. When employees and workers thrive, businesses and organizations thrive.

When employees and workers thrive, businesses and organizations thrive.

Gallup also points out that leaders must adjust to the current climate and that employees are looking for different things now.

In their study on how Millennials want to work and live, the differences are stark.

---

35 – Jim Harter and Jim Clifton, *It's the Manager: Gallup Finds the Quality of Managers and Team Leaders Is the Single Biggest Factor in Your Organization's Long-Term Success.* (Gallup Press, 2019).

The Change in Leadership	
Past	**Future**
My Paycheck	My Purpose
My Satisfaction	My Development
My Boss	My Coach
My Annual Review	My Ongoing Conversations
My Weaknesses	My Strengths
My Job	My Life

An inability or unwillingness to address these shifts in our culture will lead to a closure of business. Learning how to integrate and validate dignity is the key to better environments and better interactions. Dignity is at the core of purpose and development as well as strengths and life. These fundamental changes call us to champion the dignity of not just ourselves but of those we work with and for.

If we are to do this, we will have to choose courage and vulnerability. Courage because we will have to face our own challenges and fears. We will have to address our amygdala hijacks with a determination to act, not just react. Despite our initial responses, which may look like fight or flight, or if you are like me, a fainting goat, our focus must be to look at others with dignity. Vulnerability is required of us because you can't honestly address your shortcomings without it. Dignity implies tearing down walls between you and others so that meaningful and just interactions can occur. Without our walls and our basic defense mechanisms, we are vulnerable—vulnerable to one another in a way in which allows beauty and dignity to flourish.

Our courage will cause us to confront how our workplaces and other spaces in our culture create objects out of people. Name-calling, division, and objectification are the antithesis of dignity. When people are products, we expose ourselves to the atrocities and failures we long to avoid. This means asking those not previously invited to join us in areas previously considered off-limits. Boardrooms and meeting tables will look different because of our courage. It means we choose to dance with those who are with us, and we choose to celebrate them for the dignity they possess. It means we avoid the pitfalls of violating the dignity of others.

When we choose dignity, we become people responsible for our actions and avoid trying to make ourselves look good. Instead, we courageously deal with conflict and encourage feedback knowing that our identity is secure in our dignity. Instead of separating and objectifying, we choose to *relate*, gain *insight*, *serve* and act with *kindness* because people are worth the R.I.S.K.

Because of dignity, we get to be curious about others, wondering what they can teach us about life and what it means to be human instead of passing them by or acting indifferently to their presence. As a result, we increase our ability to lead others by gaining the critical characteristics of compassion and empathy.

* * *

Many words describe the way people want to interact with one another. They range from things like kindness to gentleness. Words like empathy and compassion are an important part of the discussion, even though they differ from dignity. We all try to grasp how we can walk next to each other and respond to one another. Each in some way falls short but engenders goodwill and concern for our fellow man.

How then are we to be together?

Aside from dignity, as this book has pointed out, let's briefly look at two other words that compliment dignity beautifully: empathy and compassion.

A Word About Empathy

What is empathy? President Barack Obama said, "Learning to stand in somebody else's shoes, to see through their eyes, that's how peace begins. And it's up to you to make that happen. Empathy is a quality of character that can change the world."

Merriam-Webster defines it as "the action of understanding, being aware of, being sensitive to, and vicariously experiencing the feelings, thoughts, and experience of another of either the past or present without having the feelings, thoughts, and experience fully communicated in an objectively explicit manner."

Putting yourself in someone's shoes, seeing things from their perspective is empathy. Why does it matter? Because no one likes to feel like an object, and no one wants to feel alone. One of the things people seek in a community is to feel understood. Misunderstandings happen all the time when we lack empathy. We make decisions without taking others into account or how they may feel about what we are doing. I am not sure what is worse: not taking them into account or taking them into account and deciding how they feel about the circumstance doesn't matter. Empathy matters. We are dealing with people, not objects. People who are moms, dads, brothers, and sisters who are doing their best to provide for themselves or their loved ones. I have said it before, and I will say it again: *It isn't just what we do; it is how we do it.*

No one likes to feel like an object, and no one wants to feel alone.

Assume you need to make a tough personnel decision that will leave someone without a job or a significantly reduced salary. Of course, no one wants to deliver that message and be the bearer of bad news. We've all heard the stories of companies and managers who deliver the news by phone call, email, Zoom, or, heaven forbid, by text message. The lack of character and empathy in the mode of delivery leaves a terrible impression and makes people feel unworthy of face-to-face interaction. They ask, "Wasn't I worth a meeting? Couldn't you tell me to my face?"

Our own lack of emotional intelligence or our inability to handle difficult feelings keep us from being present to others, especially when delivering difficult news. Through the years, I have had ample opportunity to be present to people in great distress. Being a non-anxious presence in the middle of someone else's pain is critical, whether they are facing a terrible diagnosis, relationship breakup, or a death.

I saw this firsthand in high school. One spring day in western Montana, the kind of warm day where the sun shines and sheds the cold and dreary winter gray, some fellow students left school in a hurry. Excited about a Friday afternoon and the great weather, they raced down a busy two-lane road just south of the high school. Though the details were muddled, we heard from other students there was a bad accident that involved kids I knew. Apparently, they were speeding and attempting to pass multiple vehicles at a time. The driver (who I knew) lost control and rolled the car. He wasn't wearing a seatbelt and was ejected from the car. What we knew at the time was that he was seriously injured and maybe possibly even died. No sooner did we hear this news than his dad's vehicle came racing into the school parking area.

I remember this next interaction like it was yesterday. I was standing with my track coach (who had children of his own) and watched as he interacted with the panicked dad.

"Where is Sean?" the dad asked in terror. He heard there was an accident near the school but didn't know the details, so he came to the school for information (this was before cell phones).

My coach responded, "What I know is that there has been a very serious automobile accident that apparently involves your son. It has happened just down the road. I am so sorry I don't have any more information." The pain and worry was all over my coach's face as he delivered the message, no doubt feeling the pain Sean's dad felt.

Scared and angry, the dad ran to his car and tore off down the road to the horrific scene. Aside from how sad this event was, I remember being in awe and admiration for how my coach handled that interaction. He was professional but caring and didn't allow his emotions to keep him from being present to Sean's dad. It was a moment I will never forget.

Empathy matters.

A Word About Compassion

Compassion is another word people use when describing the ways we interact with one another. As managers and companies become more aware that treating people with a whole-person approach is a much better way of leading, compassion moves to the forefront of the discussion.

> "Compassion comes into the English language by way of the Latin root 'passio,' which means to suffer, paired with the Latin prefix 'com,' meaning together—to suffer together. The concept of compassion and its link to suffering has deep philosophical and religious roots. For instance, Christian theologian Thomas Aquinas noted the interdependence of suffering and compassion when he wrote: 'No one becomes compassionate unless he suffers.'"[36]

Compassion involves empathy and the ability to be in someone else's shoes, but it goes further. Compassion involves action. Once the emotion is identified, steps

---

[36] – Jacoba M. Lilius et al., *Compassion Revealed* (Oxford University Press, 2011), https://doi.org/10.1093/oxfordhb/9780199734610.013.0021.

toward alleviating the pain or addressing the situation are compassion. Compassion International is a well-known organization that seeks to "release children from poverty in Jesus' name through a holistic approach to child development."[37] Other organizations such as Food for the Hungry and Project Cure seek to do much the same for people who suffer and possess far fewer resources than we do. We may not all feel the pull to assist in child development or tangible relief efforts, but we can still show compassion.

Have you ever taken someone out for coffee who is going through a hard time? Have you ever gently rubbed someone's back who is suffering? Ever held a child in your arms who was sick? That is compassion.

Compassion is action. It could be something as simple as writing an email to let someone know you're there for them. It could be taking someone who could use a break to lunch, or simply stopping by their desk to chat or listen. Compassion communicates to people that they matter and what they are going through matters. It says you care about them and are willing to be present to them in what they are experiencing.

Employees with compassionate bosses will walk through fire for them. I bet you are loyal to people who treat you with compassion or who were present when you needed it most. I know I am. Compassion matters everywhere, including the workplace.

Both compassion and empathy are ways in which we can "be" with each other. They imply connectedness and importance. It's meaningful for people to connect this

---

37 – Compassion International, "Releasing Children From Poverty in Jesus' Name," Sponsor a Child - Compassion International, December 4, 2018, http://www.compassion.com/about/about-us.htm.

way at the office or at play. Developing these characteristics helps us see that people aren't that different from one another, and in fact, we are a lot more alike than we admit. And this commonality gives us some cross-over relational coin. We find similarities and learn to appreciate the differences without judgment. This is why our stories are so important.

When we take time to learn one another's stories, we find places of resonance and respect. It is easy to admire someone who has overcome difficult situations with dignity and grace. Yet, we won't know those stories until we ask and listen.

What's even more beautiful is that all of our stories are still being written.

A Word About Civility

When discussing dignity, a word that continues to come up in management and leadership circles is civility. Civility is a critical component of how we interact with those we work with. It sets the stage for how we run meetings, deal with conflict, and address critical issues. In essence, civility is civil, but it isn't the same as dignity. Civility connotes civilization, meaning we are polite and civilized with one another. It seeks to provide a baseline that governs our interactions with fellow employees and anyone we come in contact with.

Civility is difficult, especially when the amygdala is triggered and one's brain tells them to act in any way but civilized. It is also tricky because no one can guarantee that those they interact with are also committed to civility. Further, society is less and less civil. It was once uncommon to see political leaders and others in high positions behaving in uncivil ways. Name-calling, angry outbursts, finger-pointing, and blaming come very easy, and social media allows anyone to act uncivilized with very little repercussion. Because uncivilized behavior is showing up in more places, it has become easier to model and much more challenging to oppose. It also means we will feel the power of dignity that much more.

Because civility is about behavior and not about identity, you can act civilly toward another and still feel contempt for them. You can be polite and still have the deepest desire for their downfall. You may be civil with those around you, but dignity demands you honor the dignity that you possess. That might be the biggest challenge you face from this book—how to identify yourself with dignity.

Civility is on the surface, and make no mistake, it is important. However, dignity is what demands civil behavior. Dignity is not just below the surface, it is above, below, and beyond. It governs the way we think, behave, and feel. Without dignity, there is very little reason to behave in a civil manner.

Empathy, compassion, and civility all have their place, and they are all important individually, but in order to overcome the objectification and the dignity disconnect at work and other places, we must dig deeper.

CONCLUSION
Becoming a Dignity Champion
Beyond Policies and Procedures

I RECENTLY ASKED DONNA HICKS if dignity possessed power in the same way that, for instance, royalty does. Her response was brilliant:

> Dignity has extraordinary power. When people claim their dignity, the internal power they achieve makes them resilient, not getting thrown off by others' attacks. Knowing we have dignity protects us from the destabilizing effects of thinking we are not worthy. If we know we are worthy, we can get through anything. Also, the power we have can empower others as well. When we treat people with dignity, we gain tremendous relational power. Using our power to empower others is what it's all about.

Every interaction we have can either validate or violate dignity. We can either close the gap or create one. When people feel their worth, they have an opportunity to overcome spaces between us that cause turn over at work, inefficiencies, loss of impact, misunderstanding, and pain. With dignity, we can be those who build bridges, not just between us and those around us, but also for others to become more than they believed they could be, 'the best version of themselves.' The path of dignity is not an easy one. It requires attention and determination. Dignity demands we constantly re-evaluate our actions, relationships, attitudes, and beliefs. We must challenge our values and processes from the boardroom to HR, the watercoolers to parking lots, Zoom meetings to emails. Making dignity the HOW to our what creates a powerful and impactful organization.

It does the same with individuals. We've seen how Jesus validated the dignity Zacchaeus possessed and the transformative power it had on him. We are bearers of that great power and empower those around us. The only way people will know of and experience their dignity is if we who affirm and believe in dignity share it with them. This might sound like pie-in-the-sky talk, but it is far too important not to share because of the transforming power available to each of us. It helps bottom lines at work, improves engagement and productivity and the way people see themselves. It reaches far beyond the nine-to-five.

Closing the dignity disconnect starts with you. You are not an object. You are not a product. You are more than you produce. It may be easy for you to say that to someone else, but living it for yourself requires courage and vulnerability. Dignity means that you embrace it for yourself, allowing the transforming power of dignity to take hold of you. When dignity's power is unleashed in you, there is no telling where it will take you or the organizations you are a part of. Tell the stories, seize the moments, create the space that makes you a dignity champion. Embrace the power you possess to close gaps, unleash those around you and lead your people in the way of dignity.

AUTHOR BIO
Bob Fabey

BOB'S MONTANAN ROOTS KEEP him practical and grounded while writing and speaking about people and the workplace. His upbringing put people before task and taught him how important relationships and communication are.

Following this trajectory, Bob has worked hard to become an effective communicator and a passionate equipper. His love for giving people skills to overcome challenges and gain new insights lead him to create Fabey Insights, an organization focusing on training, coaching, and speaking for greater workplace effectiveness. This love also caused him to create the non-profit, Dignity Wins, which is dedicated to meeting practical needs in Rwanda and around the globe.

His people-focused outlook makes him a sought after trainer, speaker and mentor in both sacred and secular settings.

He and his wife Amy have been together nearly 30 years and have two grown children, Hannah and JP, and their beloved family dog Max. They live in the greater Phoenix area.

FABEY INSIGHTS

People-focused solutions providing measurable impact to your people and your business.

Team Building

Organization Development

Strategic Planning

Training

Leadership Development

Communication Coaching

Learn more at
FabeyInsights.com

CPSIA information can be obtained
at www.ICGtesting.com
Printed in the USA
JSHW021922170123
36389JS00001B/9